TWAYNE'S WORLD AUTHORS SERIES

A Survey of the World's Literature

FRANCE

Maxwell A. Smith, University of Chattanooga

EDITOR

Blaise Cendrars

TWAS 571

Blaise Cendrars

BLAISE CENDRARS

By MONIQUE CHEFDOR

Scripps College

TWAYNE PUBLISHERS
A DIVISION OF G. K. HALL & CO., BOSTON

Copyright © 1980 by G. K. Hall & Co.

Published in 1980 by Twayne Publishers,
A Division of G. K. Hall & Co.
All Rights Reserved

Printed on permanent/durable acid-free paper and bound
in the United States of America

First Printing

Frontispiece photo of Blaise Cendrars courtesy of the
Editions Denoël, Collection Raymone Cendrars

Library of Congress Cataloging in Publication Data

Chefdor, Monique.
Blaise Cendrars.

(Twayne's world authors series ; TWAS 571 : France)
Bibliography: p. 154–61
Includes index.
1. Cendrars, Blaise, 1887–1961—Criticism and interpretation.
PQ2605.E55Z63   841'.9'12   79-25074
ISBN 0-8057-6413-5

"Les grands voyageurs sont d'abord, en une longue adolescence, de grands rêveurs. . . . Le goût des voyages relève du goût d'imaginer."

(Gaston Bachelard, *Le droit de rêver*)

Contents

About the Author

Monique Chefdor is Professor of French and Comparative Literature at Scripps College, Claremont, California and Chairman of the Modern Languages and Literatures Department. *Agrégée de l'Université*, she was born and educated in France where she taught at the University of Rennes. She also held teaching positions in Southern Rhodesia, at the universities of Exeter, England and Rochester, New York, Sarah Lawrence and Hollins College. She received a Fullbright Travel Grant in 1960 and a Graves Award prize in 1972 for research on Post Sartrian French thought. She gave numerous lectures on Twentieth century literature in France, England and the United States and is the co-author and editor of *In Search of Marcel Proust* (Ward Ritchie and Scripps College, 1973), the publication of the Claremont Colleges Proust Centennial colloquium.

Assisted by three grants from Scripps College, Professor Chefdor has undertaken extensive research on Blaise Cendrars in Europe and Brazil. She translated and introduced the later poems of Cendrars in *Complete Postcards from the Americas* (University of California Press, 1976) and made two contributions to the special issue of *Europe* on Blaise Cendrars: "Blaise Cendrars et le Simultanisme" and "Chronologie et bibliographie de Blaise Cendrars". An active promoter of Cendrarian research in the United States, she is the founding President of the Blaise Cendrars Society.

Preface

Nothing could be more suited to Blaise Cendrars than the emblem of this collection: Pegasus striding over the world's globe. For many years, the legendary image of Cendrars as a world roamer has eclipsed the variety and originality of his literary production. Recently the trend has been reversed in favor of the work which is acquiring at last its due autonomy. Although the legend constructed by Cendrars is closely interwoven with his writings, the present study will lead the reader through the labyrinth of his mythopoetic construct and project the inescapability of the creative urge in him. However fascinating the writer's life is, biographical elements are only briefly sketched insofar as they are essential to the understanding of the writer's endeavor. For this reason, *Vol à Voile* and *Une nuit dans la forêt* are merely alluded to since their analysis presents a greater psycho-biographical interest than a literary one. On the other hand minor youth writings are given full treatment because of their seminal importance in the overall assessment of Cendrars's vocation as a writer. While the total production of Cendrars is discussed, including his experiments in film making, ballet, art criticism, greater attention is given to his major poetic and prose works. Special emphasis is placed on the collections of short stories and the later writings of the tetralogy which have not yet been fully treated in English.

The overall goal of this study is not only to provide a guide to the reader of Cendrars but also to project the importance of his work within the ongoing questioning of the function of writing.

MONIQUE CHEFDOR

Claremont, California

Chronology

1887   September 1: Frédéric Sauser born in La Chaux de Fonds, Switzerland, 27 Rue de la Paix.

1895   Early schooling at the Scuola Internazionale in Naples.

1897   Attends the "Gymnasium" in Basel.

1902   Studies briefly at the "Ecole de Commerce" in Neuchâtel.

1904– Franco-German correspondent for a jeweller, Mr. Leuba,
1907   Saint Petersburg, Russia.

1907   April: returns to Switzerland. Auditor in philosophy at the University of Berne.

1908   Meets Emile Szittya at the International Fair in Leipzig.

1909   Studies medicine and philosophy at the University of Berne. Meets Fela Poznanska.

1910   April: in Brussels works as a comedian. May: audits history of music courses in Berne. July–August: Brussels and La Panne. Discovers Remy de Gourmont and writes "Le dernier des masques" (to be published in *Les Hommes Nouveaux,* 1912). October: Paris, 216 Rue Saint Jacques. Writes *Conte* and does various translations.

1911   April: returns to Saint Petersburg, Russia. Starts *Alea* (the future *Moganni Nameh*). November: sails from Libau (Poland) to New York.

1912   New York. Writes *Séquences, Danse macabre de l'amour, New York in flashlight, Les Pâques.* June: returns to Europe. July: settles in Paris. September: founds the review *Les Hommes Nouveaux* with Emile Szittya and Marius Hanot. November: *Les Pâques,* signed Blaise Cendrars. Meets Apollinaire, Robert and Sonia Delaunay. Friendship with Modigliani, Soutine, Chagall, Cocteau, Max Jacob, Arthur Cravan, Canudo, Fernand Léger.

1913   One poem of *Sequences* appears in *Die Aktion,* an article on Henri Rousseau in *Der Sturm.* April: *Séquences.* June: announces *La Prose du Transsibérien,* "the first simultaneist book." September: publication of the poem.

1913– Writes *Panama* and most of the *Poèmes Elastiques*. Some of
1914   the latter appear in *Der Sturm, Soirées de Paris, Montjoie!*
1914   April: birth of his first son, Odilon. July: joins the Foreign
       Legion. September: marries Fela Poznanska.
1915   September: wounded at the Ferme Navarin. Right arm
       amputated. December: awarded the "Médaille militaire"
       and the "Croix de Guerre."
1916   February: naturalized French citizen. April: birth of second
       son, Rémy. *La guerre au Luxembourg.*
1917   Cannes, Nice. *Profond Aujourd'hui.* Returns to Paris in
       spring. Frequents the *Café de Flore* and *La Rotonde* with
       Apollinaire, Soupault, Desnos, Aragon, Pascin, Soutine,
       Picabia, Léger, Modigliani. July: moves to La Pierre, writes
       L'Eubage for Jacques Doucet. Back in Paris in autumn,
       meets Raymone Duchateau.
1918   Nice, Paris. Works with Abel Gance on the film *J'accuse. J'ai
       tué*. Becomes a literary director of the *Editions de la Sirène.
       Panama.*
1919   Paris. *Du Monde Entier. Dix neuf poèmes élastiques. La fin
       du monde filmée par l'Ange Notre Dame.* "Modernités" in *La
       Rose Rouge*. November: prepublication of an excerpt from
       Moravagine in *Littérature*. Birth of Miriam Cendrars in
       Nice.
1920   Works with Abel Gance on *La Roue.*
1921   Rome: Studios Rinascimento. *L'anthologie nègre.*
1922   *La perle fiévreuse* and *Moganni Nameh* in periodicals. Col-
       laborates with Darius Milhaud and Fernand Léger on the
       ballet *La Création du Monde.*
1922– Moves frequently between Paris, Le Tremblay sur Mauldre
1923   and Biarritz. October 25: Théatre des Champs Elysées, first
       performance of *La Création du Monde.*
1924   February–September: first visit to Brazil (Rio, Sao Paulo,
       Minais Gerais). *Kodak (Documentaires), Le Formose.*
1925   *L'Or.* Completes *Moravagine* at Le Tremblay.
1926   January–June: second visit to Brazil (Rio, Sao Paulo).
       *Moravagine, L'ABC du cinéma, L'Eubage, Eloge de la vie
       dangereuse.*
1927   Le Tremblay, La Redonne. Works on Dan Yack.
1927– September–April: third visit to Brazil. *Petits contes nègres
1928   pour les enfants des Blancs.*

Chronology

1929 Le Tremblay, Paris, Toulon, Biarritz. *Le Plan de l'Aiguille.*
  Les confessions de Dan Yack. Une nuit dans la forêt.
1930 Paris, Biarritz, Hyères, Montpazier, brief journey to
  Portugal. Reports for *Vu* on the trial of Jean Galmot. Dos
  Passos visits him for a week in Montpazier. Founds the
  collection *Les Têtes Brûlées, Au Sans Pareil. Rhum, Comment les Blancs sont d'anciens Noirs.*
1931 Le Tremblay, Paris, trip to Spain. *Aujourd'hui, La Création du Monde.*
1932 *Vol à Voile.*
1934 Meets Henry Miller in Paris.
1935 *Panorama de la pègre.* May 29–June 3, sent by *Paris-Soir* as
  a reporter on the maiden voyage of SS Normandie from Le
  Havre to New York.
1936 January–February: Hollywood, reporter for *Paris-Soir.* Sails
  back via Panama Canal and the West Indies. *Hollywood, la
  Mecque du cinéma.*
1937 *Histoires Vraies.* Translates *A Selva* by Ferreira de Castro.
  Several trips to Spain and Portugal.
1938 *La vie dangereuse.*
1939– War correspondent in the British army. *D'Oultremer à*
1940 *Indigo. Chez l'armée anglaise.*
1940– Resides in Aix-en-Provence.
1948
1945 *L'Homme foudroyé*
1946 *La Main coupée*
1948 *Bourlinguer.* Moves to Villefranche in January.
1949 *Le lotissement du ciel. La banlieue de Paris.* October 27:
  marries Raymone in Sigriswill, Switzerland.
1950 September: settles in Paris. October 15–December 15: radio
  interviews with Michel Manoll.
1951 December 25: "Noëls du monde entier," French radio.
1952 *Le Brésil, des hommes sont venus. Blaise Cendrars vous
  parle.*
1953 *Noël aux quatre coins du monde.*
1955 In collaboration with Nino Frank, radio plays: *Serajevo*
  (January 15), *Gilles de Rais* (December 17).
1956 *Emmène-moi au bout du monde.* Summer: first attack of
  paralysis.
1957 *Trop c'est trop.* Radio play: *Le Divin Aretin* (June 1).

1958 Summer: second attack of paralysis. Named "Commandeur de la Légion d'Honneur."

1959 *Films sans images.*

1961 January: Awarded the *Grand prix littéraire de la ville de Paris.* January 21: dies Rue José Maria de Heredia.

CHAPTER 1

Mythomania / Mythopoeia

Truth is imaginary. You must not copy through a transfer paper nor write a confession. I have always made a point to commit myself in life in order to gather material for my books. Then you can have some leeway, can't you?[1]

THIS comment by Blaise Cendrars brings into focus the touchstone that exposes the relationship of the author's life to his literary creation. Time and again, in the press, in radio interviews and in his works, Blaise Cendrars defended in such a manner the veracity of the experiences which nourished his writings. When pried with personal questions he would deftly elude them and yet overwhelm his auditors with more extravagant "true stories" and convince everyone that "yes, yes, yes" he was there or here, he had gone whale hunting in the Antarctic, sailed on the Amazon, starved in New York and frozen to death in Siberia, lived among gypsies and shared a room with Charlie Chaplin when he was a juggler in a London circus. At the same time, however, dodging incredulous insistent inquirers he underscored with equal conviction that truth is always imaginary, that literature is intrinsically a poetic lie which restores truth in the eyes of the reader. In spite of his own countless derogatory comments on writing—"writing is not living," "we are not on earth to produce books" (vol. 15, p. 24)—his answer to Parinaud's interview quoted above clearly states the priority of his commitment to literature. While it asserts the importance of active involvement in life it would seem to modify, if not deny, the legendary image of the world roaming poet-adventurer now and then jotting down some notes between two ocean crossings. Moreover, when asked in another interview to sum up concisely the main characteristics of his work, his answer was even more revealing: "in one word: irrealism."[2]

Why not therefore take Cendrars at his word and dismiss all

15

attempts to reconciliate the real man with the persona he projected, to unravel truth from fiction? In this last quarter of the century when trends in criticism invite to "discard the assumption that at a certain point a subject X has produced a piece of writing," should we not let the individuality of the author disappear in favor of "the intertext in the infinite of language?"[3] Similarly when it is considered anachronistic to envisage literature as a medium of content or representations, it should be of little import whether or not the body of work we examine is the testimony of "real" experiences or the reflection of the author's personality. Such an approach would even be justified by the author's statement that "language has seduced me. Language perverted me. Language trained me. Language distorted me. That is why I am a poet. . . ." (vol. 13, p. 17)

Nevertheless Cendrars's personality has remained overwhelming and inescapable. To paraphrase Pascal, readers came to look for the writer and found the man, or, at least, thought they did. For over half a century, like Baudelaire's "children crazed with maps and prints and stamps,"[4] they have been spellbound by the "Homer of the Transsiberian,"[5] the "Marco Polo of the XXth century."[6] In the heyday of Modernism his writings seemed to be a live echo of the beat of "the prodigious centers of industrial activities, New York, Berlin, Moscow," (vol. 6, pp. 55–56) the horrors of the Russian Revolution, the dynamism of Brazil, the bewildering spell of Arctic lands as well as the new life springing forth everywhere in the arts, film industry, poetry. His stories, novels, poems, and essays have been received as a continuous confession of a hero of our time. Cendrars was seen as the epitome of the twentieth century, became the prototpye of the transnational being for whom no physical nor spiritual boundaries existed. His works were read as the living testimony to one of the most liberated lives of which people may only dream.

Does the disclosure of a different truth discard the legendary figure of Blaise Cendrars as a mythomaniac and make his work lose some of its vitality and zest? Or does it free it to a life of its own? As Claude Leroy put it, "the most famous imaginary hero created by the Swiss writer could very well be Blaise Cendrars."[7] Mythomania, a propensity for exaggerating the projection of the self, is then ruled out by mythopoeia, a deliberate reconstruction of reality through poetic vision. Recent research[8] has already pared the intricacy of Cendrars's inventions and given the work its textual autonomy. Far from dissociating the subject behind the author from the object of his works, the disclosure of the mythopoetic nature of both points to an even closer relationship between the two. The amount of "leeway" taken between actual experience and literary creation has to be determined in order to assess the creative process, yet actual life and artistic synthesis remain closely interwoven, for the work embodies a dual relationship of the self to the world.

I *Restless Youth*

Until the publication of Jean Buhler's study (1960) and the author's early diaries in *Inédits Secrets* (1969), the main source of information on Cendrars's youth has been *Vol à Voiles* published in 1932. Within the entire body of Cendrars's production this short volume appeared indeed as one of the more direct autobiographical narratives: a straightforward account of the author's reminiscences of his childhood and adolescence. Hugues Richard's recent release of Cendrars's correspondence with Sven Stelling Michaud, the publisher of *Vol à Voiles*, brought information about the circumstances of its composition which sheds a different light on the book. The letters reveal that the initial choice of the topic was not Cendrars's. It was suggested to him by the publisher. Cendrars's willingness to comply with the offer soon became hampered by his difficulty to write about himself. Following a series of letters postponing the required deadline and fourteen months after the contract had been signed Cendrars confessed:

I have been thinking a lot about *Vol à Voiles*, but have not written a line yet. I am very much afraid that the topic you chose for me troubles me deeply whenever time comes to tackle it. Stirring memories of childhood! One never knows how far it can go.[9]

Once the project was finally near completion, however, Cendrars wanted to continue the series with two more volumes and acknowledged the pleasure he took in the process: "I enjoyed myself a great deal in writing it."[10] The concept of *"divertissement"* expressed in the original French *("Je me suis beaucoup diverti")* appears even then as the core springboard for Cendrars's autobiographical writings. They are not to be read as confessions but as a playful reconstruction of a fictive image.

Nevertheless, as a mere chronology testifies, reality hardly comes short of the legend. If Blaise Cendrars was not born at 216 Rue Saint

Jacques in Paris, as he would have his readers believe, but was Frédéric Sauser, born in La Chaux de Fonds, Switzerland, on September 1, 1887, young Freddy's childhood was not unworthy of the future world roamer. The illustrious ancestry he boasts about in *Vol à Voiles*—a Renaissance humanist Thomas Platter, friend of Erasmus and Rector of the Bâle "lycée," a great uncle Leonard Euler, a famous mathematician who spent several years at the court of Catherine II, a poet and philosopher, Jean Gaspard Lavater, who invented physiognomy—is probably pure fantasy. Yet, his more humble true origins account no less for his propensity to travel and his fiercely independent temperament.

His father came from a family of Anabaptists who fled from the French Jura and settled in the small mountain village of Sigriswill in Berne County to escape the religious and political pressures of the French state. Little is known of his actual career. At the time of his wedding, he was listed in La Chaux de Fonds civic registry as a clock merchant and was probably less of an inventor than Cendrars pretended in *Vol à Voiles*. It has been ascertained that he had pursued a number of unsuccessful business ventures in various parts of Europe and in Egypt. Thus, Freddy's early years were exposed to the family's restless travelling life.

The first evidence of young Freddy's school life is at the Scuola Internazionale in Naples. In 1897, he was registered in the Bâle "gymnasium" and in 1902 enrolled at the Neuchatel business school. The famous escape, related in *Vol à Voiles*, from his parents' house to the railroad station and from there to Russia and China, has been long exposed as one of Cendrars's fabulations. It is now common knowledge that Freddy Sauser was indeed in Russia from 1904 to 1907 not, however, smuggling jewels into the far reaches of Siberia and China as he averred, but working in Saint Petersburg as a Franco-German salesman for a Swiss watchmaker, Mr. Leuba, on 34 Gorokhovaya Street.

Therefore, the eighteen-year-old future Cendrars did spend in Russia the momentous year of the 1905 Revolution which twenty years later would provide the material for some of the most forceful pages of *Moravagine*. Back home in April 1907, he enrolled as an auditor at the University of Berne where he studied philosophy and medicine. Toward the end of that year he settled on a farm near Meaux in France where he is supposed to have raised bees and grown pears. In 1908 we find him at the International Fair of

Leipzig; in 1910 he worked as a comedian in Brussels for a few weeks; in October he went to Paris and settled at 216 Rue Saint Jacques, his imaginary birthplace, until his return to Saint Petersburg in April 1911.

Although he did not go to Canada as a tractor driver and was not plying between Libau and New York in 1910 allegedly convoying immigrants from Russia, he did sail once from that Polish port to New York. The purpose of his voyage was less adventurous but no less romantic: his future first wife, Fela Poznanska, a Polish student whom he had met in Berne, was then working in New York and had sent him a ticket for his passage. He spent six months in New York from December 18, 1911 to June 1912.

The twenty-five-year-old Freddy Sauser had already travelled widely enough to justify the image of the world roaming Cendrars.

II *Paris Bohemia and the Foreign Legion*

The life which, from now on Blaise Cendrars and no longer Frédéric Sauser, led in Paris during the following years outwardly again meets the expectations set by the legend. When he startled Paris literary circles in 1912 with his poem *Easter in New York*, Cendrars's reality was beyond the fiction. He was a ubiquitous presence in the Montparnasse artists haunts: at La Ruche he met Chagall, Modigliani, Soutine, Pascin; at the Closerie des Lilas he was frequently seen with Canudo, Max Jacob; at the "Wednesdays" of Apollinaire Boulevard Saint Germain he met Sonia and Robert Delaunay, Cocteau; at the Bal Bullier he stunned the public with his extravagant American ties parading in a colorful foursome with Arthur Cravan in his paint daubed shirt-tails and the Delaunays in their "simultaneous" dresses and tuxedos.

After staying a few weeks in the studio of his brother-in-law, the painter Richard Hall, he moved to a small hotel room in the Latin Quarter Rue Saint Etienne du Mont with Emile Szittya, the founder of the German review *Neue Menschen*. A few months later, in September 1912, he founded with Szitya and Marius Hanot the review *Les Hommes Nouveaux*, establishing its headquarters in two small attics on 4 Rue de Savoie. These were also to become the print shop of the review, the office of an "International Translation Service" and for many years the "permanent" residence of Cendrars who kept the place to dump things there between trips while he was experimenting with living in every possible other section of Paris and its suburbs (Saint Cloud, Sèvres, Ville d'Avray, Les Forges, Saint Martin en Bière, etc.)

The *Hommes Nouveaux* was discontinued after three issues, but Cendrars maintained a publishing house of the same name and himself published his first poems *Pâques, Séquences,* and *La Prose du Transsibérien,* while he was scrabbling a living from translations and articles he wrote under various pseudonyms. To complete the picture of this archetypal figure of the Paris artist world in the first decades of the century, Cendrars mixed with anarchists such as the "Bande à Bonnot" whose members he frequently met at a café of the Rue Cujas, Victor Meric, author of *Comment on fera la Révolution* (1910), Victor Serge and other Russian *emigrés* revolutionaries.

When the war broke out, however, this staunch advocate of liberation who had freed himself from all family, social, national, political or spiritual fetters, and kept fiercely aloof from any literary or artistic coteries, did not resist the nation's call to action and enlisted in the Foreign Legion in August 1914. A month later he shackled his independence further with yet another social contract: he married Fela who had returned from New York in May 1913 and shared his vagabond life in the Paris suburbs. They already had a son since April and were to have a second one two years later. But Cendrars was too much at grips with the world and his own creative devouring fire to be a family man. After the war he gradually disappeared from Fela's orbit.

His war experience was dramatically curtailed within a year by the loss of his right arm during a battle in the Marne valley on September 26, 1915. If it did not actually curb the writer's talent, this ordeal was certainly to have a profound impact. The recurring theme of war in his novels and short stories and his obsession with teratology and mutilation of every kind are not a merely coincidental reflection of the spirit of the time.

III   *The Mature Creative Years: Action on All Fronts*

From now on, Cendrars's personal history seems to follow the curve of his creative life and may almost be reconstructed through the analysis of his works. It was not however restricted to recollections and imaginary transfigurations of a past or dreamed reality.

While from 1917 onwards hardly a year elapsed without a new publication from Cendrars (either articles or books), he also appeared on all fronts of the Paris art life in the 1920s: art criticism with articles on the Cubist painters in the *Rose Rouge* (1919), publishing innovations while he was the director of the Sirène (1918–1921), cinematographic experiments first with Abel Gance in 1920 and with the studio Rinascimento in Rome in 1921, new creations for the Ballets Suédois in 1923. Later in the 1930s he became a reporter for several leading Parisian daily newspapers *(Vu, Le Jour, Paris Soir)*. At the beginning of the Second World War, he once more chose public action, despite his avowed vocation for freewheeling individualism, and proudly sported the British uniform as a war correspondent for the English army.

Meanwhile his reputation for his *"bourlinguage"* (roughing it) was not entirely usurped since, during the three decades between the two world wars, Cendrars never had a permanent address. With the exception of a small country house in Le Tremblay-sur-Mauldre where he regularly took refuge to write, he mostly favored the hotel life in Paris, at times giving the address of the Alma Hotel, Ave Montaigne, at times giving that of the Sirène or the Sans Pareil publishing houses. He frequently stayed in Southern France (Cannes, Nice, Toulon), once in La Redonne, a remote fishing village near Marseilles, often in Biarritz, where he was the guest of Mrs. Errazuris, the famous wealthy South American patron of artists of the time. He also made numerous trips to Spain and Portugal.

At one point in his life he was almost a commuter between Paris and Brazil. The number of his visits to Brazil has been originally exaggerated or the fact dismissed as a pure figment of imagination. There is, however, hardly any distortion in the portrait of the eccentric international businessman intoxicated with a hundred-and-one simultaneous transactions which Nino Franck sketched in *"Instantanés de Cendrars, retour de Rio."*[11] Cendrars actually entertained for a while dreams of automobile, coffee, and fuel export-import trade, film productions in Brazil, land sales and—for three months at least—took an apartment in Paris, Rue des Marroniers, with a cable address "Cendraraym." If he did not explore the Amazon jungle or travel to the Antarctic as the legend would have it, he did make three prolonged visits to Brazil in the 1920s. His arrival in Santos on board the SS Formosa on February 6, 1924 is a matter of public record. So are the public lectures he delivered in Sao Paulo during his stay there. He returned to France on board the SS Gelria in September 1924. Similarly, his crossings to Brazil on board the SS Flandria in January 1926 and back to

France in June 1926 on board the SS Arlanza have been ascertained. Although the exact dates of his third voyage are still unknown, ample evidence of his presence in Brazil between September 1927 and April 1928 may be culled from the local press and living testimonials.[12]

Similarly, although Cendrars did not sail to New York "nine times in a row for the week-end in 1938" as he boasted to Michel Manoll during his radio interviews (vol. 13, p. 136), he was on board the Normandie as a reporter for *Paris-Soir* for her inaugural voyage from Le Havre to New York in 1935. And he definitely returned to New York in 1936 on his way to Los Angeles where he had been sent by *Paris-Soir* to work on a series of articles on Hollywood.

Cendrars undoubtedly set out more often than not on his imaginary road that strides across the ocean "from the steps of Notre Dame to its terminal point on the other side of the Atlantic beyond the Yguassu and up to the Rio Parana." (vol. 9, p. 330) As this present study will emphasize, the legendary world roamer mused as much through books in all the libraries of the world as along highways. Nevertheless, the actual life of the man held enough in stock to support the mythopoetic construct of the writer.

IV *Final Return to Paris*

The Second World War seems to have put an end to Cendrars's rampages. After resigning from his function as War Correspondent for the British Army in 1940, he withdrew to Aix-en-Provence where he disappeared from public limelight. It is very likely that these years of retreat were not as inactive or sedentary as is commonly accepted. But, as Jay Bochner points out,[13] Cendrars's known opposition to the political regime of the time would have necessitated extreme caution on his part, hence his choice for ostentatious silence. After three years of such real or pretended retreat, he took up the pen again and started to weave the web of the multitudinous vision of his last works "inserting his life into his typewriter like a carbon paper between two sheets of white paper." (vol. 11, p. 167) In 1948 he moved to Villefranche. A year later, Cendrars's most intimate and probably only true dream was realized. The mysogynist author of *Moravagine* and *Emmène-moi au bout du monde,* the man for whom "the only hope there was in love was the hope of hopelessness,"[14] was also the man who posed now and then as the Casanova of the twentieth century, leaving desper-

ate lovers in every corner of the world and on the decks of every
ocean liner. This same man at sixty-two married the one woman he
had loved through all his life with the most intense idealized
platonic love, the actress Raymone Duchateau whom he had met in
1917 and always come back to ever since.

With the exception of a few trips to Switzerland and Belgium with
his wife the story of his life in Paris from 1950 to his death in 1961
merges with that of his last creative efforts. Two attacks of paralysis
in 1956 and 1958 reduced him to near silence. Yet Cendrars
continued writing brief texts (short stories, prefaces) until his death
on January 21, 1961. By the end of his life the independent roamer
had become a publicly recognized figure in the Paris literary world
of letters: in 1958 André Malraux brought to his home the decoration of "Commandeur" of the Legion of Honor and a few weeks
before his death the city of Paris honored him with its "Grand prix
littéraire."

V   An "Inexhaustible Creative Substance"[15]

Although the margin of discrepancies between the fictive life of
this fabulous storyteller and his real biography is wide enough,
there was a sufficient variety of actual events for the poet to add to
the annals of his imagination. His claim to the truth of his adventures
is not without grounds. Yet the relationship of the author to the
mythopoetic creation of his writings is not to be found only in the
interplay between factual outer reality and the imaginative universe
of his text. The inner biography of this enigmatic figure opens up an
infinitely more complex interwoven tissue of contradictions.

Numerous testimonies from people who approached him during
his life assert that he was the man of his part: a dynamic character
overflowing with warmth, understanding, generosity, open to all—
princes as well as outlaws—buoyantly active and serene as a lama,
with a unique gift of blending past and future in the permanent
instant of the present which he lived to the fullest, freed from all
inner fetters. Yet, upon taking a closer look, behind the apparently
garrulous endless talker one finds the most reserved of men, and a
deeply tortured one. *Une nuit dans la forêt,* which he subtitled
"First fragment of autobiography," is a most revealing document in
this respect, probably the only piece of writing in which Cendrars
openly spoke about his deeper inner self. He was a man who knew
everyone but lived in profound solitude, a man who together with a

Nietzschean awareness of modern ethics, fearing neither God nor devil, nor life nor death, had an almost puritanical sense of evil and lived with an irreconcilable blend of lucidity and idealism, constantly torn between a deeply ingrown Schopenhaurian pessimism and an exalted love of life. Finally he was a man who, from his very earliest experiences in Saint Petersburg, was consumed by the urge to write.

Born with what the astrologer Conrad Moricand described as a "cosmic consciousness of the kind that characterized Balzac Whitman and Jacob Boehme,"[16] Cendrars comes through as the "inexhaustible creative substance" that Henry Miller recognized in him. He could only find his real space in the boundless world of literary creation. The very choice of a pseudonym that sums up his creative formula is significant. The phonetic mutation from "*braise*" ("embers") to Blaise and the combination of "*cendres*" ("ashes") and art or arson has been frequently mentioned. For him not only "to write is to burn alive" but "the process of writing is a conflagration which sets ablaze a whole confusion of ideas and makes associations of images flare up until it reduces them to crackling embers and falling ashes." (vol. 9, p. 45) If factual outer reality can be isolated from Cendrars's creative web, the pattern of his inner reality can only be completed through the history of his creative life: the history of an indomitable protean character who discards his personality and gets a new one in order to carefully and methodically elaborate a particular mythopoetic vision.

CHAPTER 2

The Literary Apprentice "Whirling Across the Meridians Like a Squirrel in His Cage"[1]

BEYOND strictly biographical interest, the analysis of first literary utterances that an author omits from his subsequent body of published works is usually an idle pursuit or even a somewhat indiscreet one, violating the integrity of the author's creative stance. In the case of Blaise Cendrars the publication by his daughter of his early diaries, correspondence, and first literary attempts has not only established several facts of his life. It sheds light on the character of the artist's deeply rooted vocation and on the source and development of his esthetics. While the young Freddy Sauser was "whirling across the meridians" between Paris, Saint Petersburg, and New York he was indeed like a "squirrel in his cage" locked in the cell of his soul, gnawing at every crumb of intellectual or spiritual nourishment he was carefully storing up.

I A Romantic Vagrant Scholar

The Gargantuan reading capacity of the mature Cendrars is a widely acknowledged fact. Just as with men and events, he was always seeking out the rare egregious element in the most unknown esoteric texts. If it is not surprising that the fifty-four-year-old writer filled his war years solitude of Aix-en-Provence reading Jean de Bolland's *Acta Sanctorum* in the Mejanes Library, it is more unexpected to discover that the nineteen-year-old explorer of Russia was a self-torturing sentimentalist dreamer and a studious methodical young scholar.

Instead of travel notes on Russia the 1906–1907 diaries are a methodical recording of hours spent in the Saint Petersburg Library. The first entries are composed of quotations from Lamartine,

Chateaubriand, Coleridge, typical choices for an adolescent of his generation, also notes from articles in *La Revue des Deux Mondes* and lists of readings that include Dante, Darwin, Durkheim, Taine as well as La Bruyère, a study on Richard Wagner and *L'astronomie populaire* by Camille Flammarion. The fascination that this volume exerted on the young Freddy is already most informative in relation to the future writer whose explorations were not to be limited to the geographical boundaries of this planet.

After his return to Neuchatel in May 1907 lists of twelve to fifteen titles appear every month until he started recording his readings by alphabetical order in an indexed notebook. Despite his alleged contempt for academic education and intellectual grubbers he was meticulously compiling masses of literary and factual material which a Renaissance Humanist would not have spurned. A representative selection of titles would include most major French writers from the Middle Ages to the Symbolists, among them Villon, Rabelais, Molière, Saint Amant, Restif de la Bretonne, Nerval, Baudelaire, Rimbaud, Théophile Gautier, Huysmans and Remy de Gourmont; Greek ancient literature (mainly Homer and Orphic poems); English, German, and Russian authors such as Goethe, Poe, E. Brontë, Tolstoy, Dostoevsky, Turgenev; philosophical essays from Malebranche to Schopenhauer, Nietzsche and Bergson; works of mystics and saints (Saint Ambroise, Saint Augustine, Saint Bernard, Saint Bonaventura as well as less known ones such as Alaris de Liole and Adam de Saint Victor); treaties on a variety of unrelated subjects such as cosmetography, entomology, physiognomy, hypnotism, ancient mythology and popular culture, Christian iconography, musicology, Egyptology, medieval history of art as well as history of fashion. In less than five years, he had already accumulated enough material to provide for the world inventory of his future works.

The future Cendrars seems to have escaped more in time through his avidity for erudition than in space through his travels. Similarly, instead of a bold and carefree explorer of the world, his letters reveal a hypersensitive, exceedingly analytical introspective young man who feels "terrified by the hideous face of humankind" (pp. 149–50) and "immerses /his/ entire self in books and studies to combat the spleen that overwhelms /him/." (p. 9) Even his most intimate letters or diary jottings are selfconsciously bookish. The romantic outcries of his letters to Helene are impregnated with his readings of Lamartine and Coleridge: "I am, I exist, I live because I suffer. Suffering is the essence of my life." (p. 14) The accidental death of Helene who was burnt alive in Saint Petersburg when Freddy was back in Switzerland drew from him an authentic heart rending cry of anguish: "I spit on life which does not listen to life." (p. 29) But two years later, while his agony was still so acute that he wrote to his brother he had lived through everything life held for him and wonders what prevents him from pulling the trigger of his pistol, he acknowledged that he was writing under the influence of Richard Wagner's *Tristan and Isolde*, for he "had deeply lived" all that this music expressed. (p. 38–39). Holding a mirror to his tormented divided self, he did not seem however to be merely watching himself live in a juvenile spell of self-identification. He was already primarily intent on finding the proper means of expression for the tumultuous life that he thought was assailing him and, for lack of his own medium, searched for parallels in the creative expression of others.

The travel notes he wrote on his journey from Saint Petersburg to New York are most striking in this respect. Engaged throughout the train ride to Libau in a dialogue with "his soul sitting in front of him in the other corner" (p. 153) he admits to himself: "if it were easier to write in a train I would be ready to spend all my life in them, facing myself in front of a lighted candle." (p. 155) Yet, while the train rushes through the monotonous plains of Northwest Russia he compares the landscape and the rumble of the train's wheels to the prose of Maeterlinck he is reading at the moment and the next day thinks that Rembrandt, Beardsley, and Whistler would best express this endless succession of plains. Two days later in Varsovia, after a few brief remarks on the city, his mind wanders to the means of expressing the spirituality of the hand (a traditional Symbolist theme) and after evoking Verlaine, Rodin, Bourdelle, he dreams of ways of introducing it in the theater. Once on board the SS Birma, he notes with disappointment that "upon leaving the land he did not feel the emotion of which so many travellers speak" (p. 165) and lucidly concludes: "Why start on a journey; I am too much on the watch for myself; I need stage sets." (ibid.) A violent hurricane provides him with the ideal theatrical background: proud of his self-controlled dandy's superiority over the seasick mass of passengers, in the midst of the storm he reads Goethe's *Dichtung und Wahrheit* to "open to him the gateway to dream, all the paths that lead far away, out of the haze of consciousness." (p. 171) Although he "feels quite ridiculous with his notebook" (p. 176) while the crew is fighting the worst storm they ever had in twenty six

years, he goes on recording every impression, evoking Baudelaire's
prose poem *"Déjà,"* comparing the open sea to the Alps painted by
Segantine, reciting to himself a page from Remy de Gourmont and
figuring out which musicians would be attuned to this scenery.
Inner subjective reality still supersedes the awareness of external
multiplicity which the future writer will fuse into his mature works,
but it is already obvious that whatever the future poet lived, saw, or
did only interested him insofar as it would eventually become
written matter. Towards the end of his crossing (Dec. 8, 1911) he
clearly stated the nature of his ambition:

All this (the variety of the seascape) does not escape me now, I observe, I
notice, I feel it all; but my eyes are not accustomed to it; it is too new; I
could not capture with words all the shades and nuances of every hour; I am
too frequently bewildered. (p. 193)

Like Sartre's hero in *Nausea*, Roquentin, he knows that there may
not be any adventure unless one starts recounting even the most
banal event, but for the future Cendrars the choice between living
or telling is already made, or rather there is no such choice, for
living for him is telling.[2]

II   *In Search of a Medium: Frédéric Sauser Gradually Becomes Blaise Cendrars*

Young Frédéric Sauser did not limit his literary apprenticeship to
personal diaries and reading notes. Before he chose to launch Blaise
Cendrars as a poet with his 1912 publication of *Les Pâques* he had
tried his hand at various prose and verse experiments and was
already asserting his writer's vocation.
    Since no trace so far has been found of *Novgorode la légende de
l'or gris et du silence*[3] the first example of the preCendrars manner
is a 1910 text entitled *Conte* (pp. 57–102), the phantasmagorical
account of a dream related in a fashion that less foreshadows
Surrealism than it recalls the Decadents. The theme of the hallucinatory reverie is set by a poem on Adonis which the narrator,
dozing over an ancient book in a romantic pose by a window seat, has
found inscribed inside the binding of the volume he had just let fall
on the floor. The legend of Adonis in love with a marble statue
makes such a violent assault on his imagination that for "minutes,
hours and days" he becomes "the prey to the hallucinating death

throes of a drowning man." (p. 60) Now, as himself, now identified with Adonis he goes through the stages of a nightmarish initiatory journey in which the arsenal of ancient and Christian myths, medieval symbols, gothic horrors is brought out in a surfeiting jumble. After being taken into a sensuous embrace by an octopus with the enticing lips of a woman, he sees his head riveted to a wall by a rusty nail, linked to his dismembered putrefied body by a single nerve. His heart jumps out like a bubonic toad, and every possible archetypal species of insect and worms whirl around him in a grim saraband. Lured into the sea by feminine creatures who might be Greek sirens or Slavonic Rusalkas, he finally lands in a dark Teutonic forest; he emerges from it into mysterious warm and calm woods which recall Broceliande's realm. His Odyssey continues through landmarks of religious history—Moses's land, Eurythee's kingdom, the crypts of Egyptian pyramids—to a little cottage, amusingly typical of the French countryside, in which Christ and his twelve apostles are seated at the Last Supper. Exposed later to the evils of modern city life in a luxurious brothel he finally enters a palace where "the radiant beauty of a woman's bust appeared. . . . This bust was the very beauty of love." (p. 98) Not able to resist his passionate desire, he gives the statue "the infernal kiss of resurrection" and falls amidst the statue's debris as if struck by lightning, to wake up blind by the roadside, outside the city, where, like Oedipus, he is met by his daughter.

This medley of fantasy and erudition which stemmed from all his readings of Greek mythology and ancient Slavic, German, and Sicilian tales may seem, at first, totally unrelated to Cendrars's subsequent production. He had just translated *La messe des morts* by Stanislas Przybyszewski (a Polish writer who was himself very much attracted by Huysmans and Barbey d'Aurevilly) and had evidently not yet freed himself from the influence of the late nineteenth-century tradition of satanism and cerebral eroticism. Yet a psychoanalytical interpretation of the total body of Cendrars's work would quickly bring out the recurrence of symbols and archetypes already present in this clumsy adolescent first essay. The schizoid ambivalence that underlies this text is only too transparent. On the one hand the young Sauser had not yet come to terms with his Manichean idealism, on the other it is significant that the future artisan of his own myth first explored the inner realm of his unconscious psyche through the archetypal paths of traditional symbology.

His initial fascination for the mythical lore of the past would soon lead him to view the writer as an essential feature of modern mythology and realize that his creative endeavor would inevitably entail the elaboration of a legend. In the article he wrote on Remy de Gourmont[4] in the same year, his position is firmly stated:

One of the most characteristic features of genius is probably that need to create one's own legend. Like children, the genius, this greatest child of all, wants to dream of stories in which he is the hero. This is what Nietzsche called the will to power. . . .

The genius coming into contact with the man is a puppet or a toy in his hands. He is the rag doll in the act. I never tamper with legends. It is the way in which geniuses (and Gods) come into communion with mankind. (pp. 54–55)

And only a year later Frédéric Sauser was already uncannily aware of the nature of the legendary status Blaise Cendrars would acquire. In the midst of his introspective musings on board the train which took him from Saint Petersburg to Libau, memorizing a quotation from the Latin poet Ausone, he noted:

Thus I also want a literature that exalts life, while life, in fact, I despise utterly, helpless, voluptuous, sensitive to cold and delicate as I am. Therefore thousands of howling dogs will rush along my tracks, will stupidly want to live my dreams, think my thoughts. The beasts; they will all be annihilated, and reduced to ashes, and my work is already illuminated, my pages glow somberly from the infernal blaze of the damned! (p. 160)

Such statements leave no doubt as to the character of his vocation as a writer, or the duality of his relationship to his work. While still groping for an original medium he had already set his course. Just before embarking on board the Birma, instead of the exhilaration expected from a young man starting on his first long sea voyage, the last thought he recorded is a concern for his creative future: "At the last minute, I think of Remy de Gourmont, the literary Paris, publishing business—of all a future of work, publications, articles." (p. 164)

Far from deterring the young apprentice from his literary pursuit, the ocean crossing and the arrival in New York seem to have strengthened his determination and made him take the first decisive step towards his writer's career: four days after his arrival in New York the name Blaise Cendrart (changed a year later to Cendrars) appears as his signature to a text entitled *Hic, Haec, Hoc.* (pp. 195–200). For the first time too we witness a rupture of style. Instead of the soul searching diaries of Freddy, the newborn Blaise Cendrart gives us four incisive witty sketches of people he had just met in New York: an unproductive professor drained by the routine of teaching and the burden of daily life; an unimaginative frustrated playwright who grubs for his living as an insurance agent; the lewd girls of a paltry brothel trained to maintain a front of pseudo respectability in their puritan schoolgirlish drab attire; a stupid ignorant painter who has hardly heard of the major masters exhibited in all museums and paints methodically like a watchmaker. The inward drawn epigone of dandyism has turned his look outward and discovered the art of the immediate seizure of things that will characterize Cendrars's future writings. Several notations in the New York diaries already foreshadow the verbal postcard technique he will develop fifteen years later. The following description from *Séjour à New York* of a vista between the skyscrapers, for instance, could easily number among the poetic snapshots of *Documentaires* as well as many other passages from "New York in Flashlight":

> Suddenly the skyscrapers split and, framed in steel beams I see liners tossed on the billows, islands in bloom like fierce kisses, in oceans of gold, under splendid skies. These vistas wear me out. The walls crush me more than ever and life, utilitarian life, grabs me with a hook; a crane lifts me jiggling at the end of a chain and drops me into delivery vans that unlatch. . . Away. . . ." (p. 200)

The style is not yet entirely stripped of metaphorical excess, but the future poet has already learned how to set the telescopic lens of his mind on the significant detail that suggests the whole.

The choice of his manner, however, was not yet determined, for during the next months he completed the series of poems entitled *Séquences*, which he published in 1913 but rejected later from his complete works as "a sin of youth."[5] Composed in the same style as the poem entitled *"Figure de rêve. Séquence"* which Remy de Gourmont's hero Entrargues writes in the novel *Sixtine*,[6] these love poems are but an exercise in Symbolist versification. Although Cendrars's verses are more sensuous and more daring than the aerial lines of De Gourmont, erotic passion evoked in traditional metaphors of blood, fire, and thunder is opposed to the "white wings" of innocent spiritual desire and there are more echoes of

Baudelaire and Verlaine than traces of Cendrars's own inspiration. This is not yet a case of intertextual play in the tradition of parodic or collage use of texts which has become the hallmark of a certain form of modernity in the wake of Surrealism. It is still simply a classic example of pastiche in recognition of his acknowledged master.

At the same time, and in a similar vein, Cendrars tried his hand at playwriting. Instead of American motifs one might expect to inform his writing during that New York stay, a Chattertonian theme inspires the short drama *Danse macabre de l'amour*. It overflows with Romantic and Symbolist clichés. The hero, Daudentley, a young writer (handwritten pages scattered on a table indicate the nature of his calling), is a perfect Romantic stereotype: tall, gaunt, pale, garbed in a black velvet robe lined with gold brocade, he has been living in total seclusion and despondency since the death of his beloved Mirja. He is first seen sitting at a piano with his head leaning on his right hand while his left hand wanders listlessly over the keyboard. He becomes enmeshed in the snares of rivalry between Mirja's mother (a woman of carnal passions, ironically called Mrs. Nadajel—which in Russian means "I am fed up with you") and her sister, Roja, who worships Daudentley with an idealized spiritual love. His fervent retort, "I want to go away; I am an artist, I want to go away," recurs like a leitmotiv throughout the play which dramatizes his struggle to leave them both. When Roja commits suicide with the gun he had just dropped on the table, he is overcome by the responsibility for another victim of "pure love" and falls down in a state of stupor, stretched on the floor under the table muttering; "I come . . . I go . . . ."

With the exception of the abundant and careful stage directions which point to Cendrars's occasional involvement in the future with the performing arts, this immature playwriting experiment hardly marks a step forward in the genesis of the writer whose inspiration is still cluttered with literary reminiscences and self-dramatization. It is, however, psychologically most revealing of his obsession at the time and his unwavering will to admit no impediment to his writer's destiny. Daudentley's creator was also the man who had been brought to New York by his lover and future first wife, Fela, and who, six days after completing the play, in a letter alluding to the "troubles" he caused her, wrote to her:

. . . I have some cyanocalium. . . . I love you. I give it to you. As to me, I don't dare yet. I have a lot to do and I will carry it out. Poverty and starvation will not keep me from writing. . . . (p. 209)

III   *The Literary Apprentice as a Hero:* Moganni Nameh

The most revealing document on these years of creative self-discovery, which finally compelled Frédéric Sauser to become the writer Blaise Cendrars, is the short narrative *Moganni Nameh* published only in 1922 but originally conceived and written in 1911 and 1912 with the title *Alea.* [7] A seemingly autobiographical account of Freddy's return to Saint Petersburg in 1911, this so-called "novel" is really a projection of the budding author's inner drama of nascent creativity, the mental odyssey of the apprentice writer.

From the very first pages, the initial objective tone of the description of Saint Petersburg gives way to the inner landscape of the split personality of the hero José who becomes the external observer of his creative life. "Following with his inner eye the play of his thoughts," he realizes the absurdity of his return to Russia. "Humiliated because he did not understand sooner that since his vital function was to write he should rather have used that overflow of energy to add three lines to an immortal poem," (vol. 4, p. 6) he embarks on an inward voyage across his inflamed imagination. It is a succession of alternating descent into sober lucidly observed reality and ascent into a world of uncontrolled dreams and fantasms. Walking on Easter day through the streets of Saint Petersburg described in terse Balzacian details he enters a remote chapel where hallucinatory visions assail him as he looks at an icon of the Virgin Mother. In a Surrealistic mixture of the sacred and the profane this "Celestial Mother" appears to him with cruel distorted sensuous lips, her long garment encrusted with the blood of menstrual flow instead of Christ's blood. Seeking solace from the Mother, the poet—identified with Christ in agony—instead of the hope of resurrection sees nothing but a "face of uncertainty and fear," which leaves him in darkness, the slab on which he was kneeling opening up under him like a grave. This symbolic entombment of the poet precedes the crucifixion scene of the next chapter. According to the regular pattern of alternation which characterizes the narrative progression, moments of lucid rational assessment of his goal as a writer, while he methodically classifies his notes, are followed by fits of imaginary creative ecstasy when José sees himself conducting the adagio for which "he must create a literary paraphrase." (p. 28) Torn between the erotic voluptuousness of the creative act and its castrative effect, unable to master all the lives he has created, he sees his whole being shattered, dismembered, his sex like "a cut up snake wriggling at his feet" while "as though spiritualized" his spirit "rises, rises, rises again" until "panting, his body horribly mangled" he falls prone in the posture of crucifixion. (pp. 25, 26, 27)

Continuously drifting from wakeful consciousness to trancelike fits of dizziness he continues to watch himself in the mirror of his creativity, now seeking inspiration in the reading of books in the library or the contemplation of paintings in the museum, now plunging back into his self-induced hallucinations, but not yet able to channel the overabundant wealth of his imagination. Although, in moments of theorizing lucidity José marvels at the way in which life and literature are closely intertwined, the way in which "mind, soul and sex are but one . . ." (p. 34), he does not find this unity in the creative act which brings him at the same time "the strongest voluptuousness" but leads to the "most utter desolation." (p. 39) Crucified on the altar of his imagination, José finds no true vital resurrection.

In her analysis Mrs. Bozon Scalzitti has revealed the source of this dualistic Symbolist ideology.[8] In theme, content, and style *Moganni Nameh* is almost entirely "lifted" from Remy de Gourmont's novel *Sixtine.* De Gourmont's hero, Entragues, like José, is a "man of letters" who despises the crowds and places art above life. Both are ridden with the same Schopenhaurian subjective idealism. They keep in their notes every line that comes to their mind, including letters they write to their lovers, are intoxicated by their readings and feel a "shiver" of joy when ordering a good book in a library. The literary references that clutter *Moganni Nameh* on almost every page (Goethe, Nerval, Descartes, Baudelaire, Lautréamont, Huysmans, etc.) are almost like those of De Gourmont. In both cases the narrative is interwoven with the literary productions of the hero-writer: two poems from *Séquences,* which, as we already pointed out, were inspired by Cendrars's reading of De Gourmont, are inserted among José's poetic attempts. The overabundance of stereotypical imagery ("the ardent rose of love," the "pale hands," the "white horse," the moon, tumultuous ocean, precious stones) as well as a propensity for using allegorical personifications of the self are also standard features in De Gourmont's works.

The parallels between *Sixtine* and *Moganni Nameh* are endless, and confirm once more that Cendrars's vocation grew out of Frédéric Sauser's readings. In fact, a number of implicit and explicit references in this early narrative as well as several evocations of Remy de Gourmont in Cendrars's later works acknowledge his debt to the master of his youth. But the analogy between José and Freddy is even more arresting. The most interesting part of this convulsive exploration of the self is the struggle of the apprentice-writer in his quest for the source of his art, which was already reflected in the early diaries with the same dualism. José's efforts to mold himself into a writer point clearly in two directions and indicate that this apparently imitative exercise of a novitiate actually was an exercise of liberation. The flights into the oceanic depths of his psyche fed by his readings, his artistic and musical knowledge as well as his hallucinations alternate with moments of realistic ironical and terse seizure of life through the observation of the external world. Similarly, while he cannot resist his overabundant verbal fertility in his moments of fantasy, he knew at the same time that:

he was still a novitiate, feeling his way, seeking. . . . he had to watch his thoughts; an intempestive metaphor took you God knows where since he had landed, bewildered, in Russia. . . . duped by . . . thoughts and images revolving around the idea of the "travelling poet" and rising to the status of a myth. (p. 5)

"Art is born from life only through a former art," wrote Malraux, "This is why every artist starts with a pastiche. This pastiche through which genius, clandestine furtively comes forth. . . ."[9] The case of this tortured portrait of the young man as an artist is a typical illustration of Malraux's statement. Through a double parodic exercise (parody of another corpus of literary creation and parody of the creative self: intertextuality versus intersubjectivity) Cendrars had not only taken the first steps toward finding a language of his own, he had also blueprinted the main lines of tension for his entire work.

CHAPTER 3

"Poetry Dates from To-Day"[1]

IN the few years preceding the First World War, as Raymond Bellour put it, Europe was a "vast poetry laboratory."[2] In Germany, Expressionism was in full swing with Berlin reviews like *Der Sturm* and *Die Aktion* promoting avant-garde writers and artists from all over Europe. Ezra Pound had been in London since 1908 leading the Imagist movement, while soon after launching the first Futurist Manifesto in Paris (February 20, 1909) the Italian poet Marinetti was invited to Moscow and Saint Petersburg where Khlebnikov's Cubo-Futurism was soon to eclipse Acmeism. A revolutionary spirit was equally animating the literary circles of Prague and Zurich where Dada originated a few years later. Paris in the meantime was a crucible of "isms." In literature alone, to mention only a few of them, Jules Romains's Unanimism, Henri Martin Barzun's Dramatism, Nicolas Baudoin's Paroxysm, Arthur Cravan's Machinism, Canudo's Cerebrism, the *Fantaisistes* with Klingsor, Francis Carco, Henri Hertz, and the early Apollinaire, the Impulsionists, Paul Fort and André Salmon's group of the Closerie des Lilas vied with each other to capture the new rhythm of modernity. As early as 1900 Supervielle had brought to Paris his nostalgia for the South American pampas. Valéry Larbaud's Barnabooth had been singing of ocean liners and transcontinental trains since 1908. Apollinaire was already famous as a "European traveller" (*"Le passant de Prague," "l'élégie du voyageur aux pieds blessés," "les onze mille verges"*). The United States and China had partly inspired Claudel's *Cinq grandes odes* (1910). In 1912 Segalen had brought *Stèles* back from China, poems suggested to him by Chinese steles and historical texts.

Therefore, when the twenty-five-year-old newly born Blaise Cendrars settled in Paris in September 1912, he found a natural nurture ground for the character of the wandering poet that he projected. His whole being was vibrating with a twentieth-century Whitmanian song of the universe, full of the accelerated mechanical beat of "New York, Berlin, Moscow, the prodigious centers of industrial activity," "the new life," "the universal lyricism." (vol. 6, pp. 55–56) Although nothing indicated it when he sailed back to Europe in June 1912, his trunks full of manuscripts which he was "ready to throw to the rabbits" (I.S. p. 210), he swept through the poetic climate of the epoch like a meteor. In spite of numerous affinities with his contemporaries, he remained fiercely independent from all coteries and literary schools, taking on immediately the proud stance of a loner. After publishing, at his own *"Edition des Hommes Nouveaux," Les Pâques* in November 1912 and *La Prose du Transsibérien* in November 1913, he declared in *Panama*, written towards the end of 1913, that "Poetry starts to-day." Was this aggressive statement a petulant dismissal of his predecessors and possible rival contemporaries or was it the expression of his personal intent of radical renewal? During the next decade he will stake out new ground with each poem until, disenchanted with the "spiritual misunderstanding and mental confusion" fostered by "the poetry that was prevailing in Paris" (vol. 9, p. 191), he will turn to prose writing and other artistic endeavors.

I   *The Agony of the Poet's Birth to the Modern World:*
Pâques à New York

The story traditionally associated with the composition of the first published work of Cendrars befittingly cast around it a Romantic halo of divine afflatus. According to Cendrars's own words in his radio interviews with Robert Manoll, the poem would have been written in a flash of inspiration, after a long solitary wandering through New York City on Easter Sunday. Having nowhere to go, since the Forty-second Street New York public library was closed, he would have entered a church (most likely Saint Bartholomew's on Park Avenue) where Haydn's *Creation* was being played. Returning later to a cold and lonely room, starved and exhausted, he went to bed and, prompted by a sudden impulse, got up, wrote the poem in a flash and went back to bed:

I had written *Les Pâques à New York* as I published it. There were three words crossed out. . . . (vol. 13, p. 159)

Whether this moving account is to be credited to the poet's mythmaking talent or not, the work resounds with a strikingly personal note and the change in 1919 from the more universal 1913 title of *Les Pâques* to *Pâques à New York* may, in fact, indicate Cendrars's desire to stress the relationship of his poem to a certain moment and place in his life. The young writer's inner crisis must have been intensified by the contrast between his experience of the "New World" in New York and all the literary and spiritual traditions in which he had been brought up.

Vibrant with the simplicity of a prayer, the long incantatory poetic sequence is an abortive attempt to relive Christ's passion as the poet walks downtown Manhattan on Easter night, seized by the absence of Christ in the modern world. For him Christ is a historical figure he only knows from ancient books, religious hymns, relics in churches, paintings in museums. The much quoted line: "I know all the Christs hung in museums,"[3] is tinged, in context, with despondency that the remembrance of all the miracles he has heard about but did not witness, only deepens. While a flicker of spiritual disquietude makes him feel the "sad and nude" call of the "Eternal," he is aware that faith belongs to past ages, and cannot touch him:

> When I was a child I never prayed.
> I did not know you then,—or now, I guess.

Yet an expectancy of spiritual surrender alternates with images of failed belief. In the Godless modern city where windows are splashed with the blood of prostitution and withered flowers are upturned chalices, the poet still sees Christ nevertheless as a symbol of dazzling light over the squalor and wretchedness of the streets:

> Your side wide open is a sun in the dark
> And your hands everywhere are flickering with sparks.

Within the core of the poem, Christ assumes a talismanic potency of presence in the repeated litany-like invocations of Him. Walking along the docks, through the Jewish ghetto, the red light district, the Bowery, Chinatown, the poet implores Christ to take pity on those modern lonely crowds, but remains unable to totally identify with Him and fulfill urban man's need for His love. While he observes the immigrants huddled on the landing piers like a herd of starving dogs, the fugitive Jews, the loose women drowning their vice in rum, the bums who cannot even afford the price of a rope to hang themselves, his impulse of Christian compassion is stalled by a typically modern disassociation of self from others. His is the modern subjective recording of human suffering, the inability to feel moral passion. He cannot love as Christ would ("I'd like to be You to love the whores") and the only comfort he offers derelicts is to help them die rather than live ("I gave him some opium so he'd get to paradise quicker").

As the inner tension of the work builds up, however, the appeal to Christ remains futile and the earlier image of light becomes the glitter of gold in the banks where Christ's blood has coagulated. The luminous presence, in an irreverent modern turnabout, is now transformed into an *"effroyable drôle"* who follows him menacingly along the street and, instead of knowing metaphysical dread, the poet is left alone with nothing but physical fear. A kind of wry resignation to God's absence from the modern world marks the watershed of that itinerant spiritually unnerving night:

> Lord, since You aren't King anymore nothing's changed very much.
> Evil has turned your cross into a crutch.

Briefly the initial nostalgia for the past ages of faith flares up again only to be extinguished by the poet's certitude that they cannot be recalled.

Identifying with Christ in his solitude he turns to the Virgin Mary but finds no support. The oncoming of dawn does not bring him any release either. The denial of new life is complete. Instead of an image of rebirth, another vision of a mutilated Christ sears his mind:

> The sun is Your Face all sullied with spit.

On the day of Resurrection the thought of Christ's entombment is brought back by the poet's withdrawal to his lonely room symbolically evoked as a grave. Calling in vain once more upon God to exorcise the spiritual nothingness of the modern age, the poet finally retreats to a preoccupation with self; a contemporary stance, inde-

pendent and detached, dictates the last line in which the mere
thought of Christ is simply dismissed:

> I think no more of You. I think no more of You.

Despite the modernity of tone in the final section, the drama
wrung out of spiritual disquietude in *Pâques à New York* first strikes
the reader as a timeless universal one which thematically evokes
such masters as Villon, Baudelaire, Verlaine, Rilke, Jehan Rictus,
and Claudel. Stylistically, it is equally steeped in tradition. The
unmetered loosely rhymed couplet, chosen by Cendrars and also
used in Paul Claudel's earlier poems, can be traced back to the
sequential poetry of the medieval monks of Saint-Gall and the poets
translated by Remy de Gourmont in *Le Latin mystique,* a source
clearly acknowledged by the initial quotation placed at the beginning of the poem. Many lines in the more modern descriptions of
the poorer districts of the city are direct echoes of Jehan Rictus's
Soliloques du pauvre (1895–1903). Villon's *"Ballade des dames du
temps jadis"* is deliberately recalled in the following couplets:

> Where are the long offices, the beautiful hymns?
> Where are the liturgies, the sweet anthems?
> Where are your proud prelates, where your little nuns?
> Where are those friends of the saints, the white dawns?

The imagery, too, harks back to the past. We find a number of
images in the Symbolist tradition: the "white dawn," "the pale
lamps," "dawn as cold as a shroud," the whiteness of hands, for
instance. In form, just as in content, the poem acquires a certain
degree of modernity only toward the end when the poet, having
resigned himself to the godlessness of the modern world, describes
the rising of the city at dawn in such startlingly modernistic lines as:

> The elevated grumbles, leaps, sways, and strains.
> The bridges shake with the railway trains.

Paradoxically enough, *Pâques à New York* has been singled out by
the critics for its resemblance to Apollinaire's "Zone," the first poem
of *Alcools* (1913), generally considered the decisive break of French
poetry into Modernism. The literary polemic triggered off by the
analogy between the two poems has lasted over half of the century

and still remains unsettled.[4] From this perspective, an extensive comparative study of the two poems has been made by Marie Jeanne Durry (see note 4). In spite of many similarities, none of which are more striking than numerous ones to be found between most poets of that period, the differences in mood, inspiration, tone, and structure are too fundamental to question the authenticity of each work. Far from echoing Apollinaire's advocacy of the religion of modernity ("You are weary at last of this ancient world," the famous first line of "Zone" which became the rallying cry of all Modernist poets), Cendrars was still only hovering on the threshold of twentieth-century sensibility. *Pâques à New York,* which has been deservedly described as "one of the nearest to perfection poetic compositions a poet has brought out in a very long time,"[5] remains a classic lyric. It is an irreducible personal cry of anguish and fear expressing the agony of the poet's birth to the modern world. Both in form and in content, Cendrars's first published poem is best read as a nostalgic farewell to his spiritual and poetic heritage. His entry into the contemporary world came with his next poetical work.

II   *The "First Simultaneous Book":*
Prose du Transsiberien et de la petite Jehanne de France

Prose du Transsibérien achieved instant fame throughout Europe even before its publication.

In February 1913, Cendrars made the acquaintance of the Simultaneist painters Robert and Sonia Delaunay. From that meeting emerged one of the most original publishing ventures of the time. Printed in Cendrars's *"Editions des Hommes Nouveaux"* in various fonts of different colors *Prose du Transsibérien* was presented as a two-meters-long folding sheet of twelve panels illustrated with the "simultaneous colors" of Sonia Delaunay Terk, and labelled "First Simultaneous book." As early as April 1913 the advanced order publicity brochure (also illustrated by Sonia Delaunay) had already aroused the hostility of the press and triggered off one of the most picaresque and violent controversies which became known as the "Polemic of Simultaneism." The debate, which initially engaged the defenders of Henri Martin Barzun, author of *Le chant dramatique simultané,*[6] against Cendrars and Sonia Delaunay, soon involved Apollinaire and the Futurists, and spread as far as Berlin. For the mere use of the word "simultaneous" on his title page, Cendrars had been accused of plagiarism, but by 1914 the claims for priority in the discovery of Simultaneism were so numerous that the critic Jean Jacques Bois from the newspaper *Gil Blas* finally closed the discussion in July 1914 with the humorous conciliatory remark:

In the future, it would be established that Simultaneism was born simultaneously, at the same hour, on the same day, in the judiciary of all Simultaneists.[7]

As Léon Somville and Pår Bergman have demonstrated at length, Cendrars's poem had nothing in common with the literary "Simultaneism" of Henri Martin Barzun, which aimed at "singing all the voices, all the passions, all the presences, all the forces of this life and this universe" simultaneously through a "polhymnic" technique very much akin to the chorus of ancient Greek theater.[8] Cendrars himself consistently advanced that the Simultaneism of his book was purely pictorial, a representation, solely made up of the "simultaneous contrasts of the colors and the text." (I.S. pp. 363–64) An analysis of the poem, however, reveals a deep inner sensitivity to the simultaneous reality of the modern world, a Heraclitean concept of unity in the interdependence of opposites.

Prose du Transsibérien, described by John Dos Passos as the "Homeric hymn of the railroad,"[9] is not only the successive narrative of the odyssey of the transSiberian railroad from Moscow to Kharbin; it is also the poet's first attempt to capture the prismatic reality of the modern world in its multiplicity.

Written in completely free verse, in which a few head and end rhymes and inner assonances alone mark a departure from prose[10] and relying for poetic effect on the mere strength of the word and images, the poem presents a study in contrasts. From the start, past and present, space and time are polarized and juxtaposed. Steeped in the now of his ardent adolescence in Moscow, at sixteen he has already forgotten his childhood because he is "16000 leagues away from /his/ birthplace."[11] At the same time, the author-narrator is still attracted to a more remote past: "My eyes were illuminating ancient paths." While evoking the spiritual peace of an old monk:

> An old monk was reading me the legend of Nizhni Novgorod
> . . .
> And I was deciphering runic letters.

he is possessed with a frenzy of destruction and revolution:

> I would have liked to grind up all the bones
> And tear out all the tongues
> And dissolve all those tall bodies naked and strange
> under garments that enrage me
> I could sense the coming of the great red Christ of the
> Russian Revolution.

Further along, struck by the incongruity of clashing events happening simultaneously in different parts of the globe, the poet contrasts the devastating images of war in Siberia with the trivial commercial pursuits of merchants transporting their goods while sardonic descriptions of prostitutes alternate with evocations of coffins and death on the battlefield.

When the narrator of the odyssey boards the train to Siberia the antinomian perception gives way to an interplay of imaginary dreams and reality. The process of fabulation takes over when the evocation of his legendary trip with the jewel merchant merges with allusions to Jules Verne's stories and the tale of Alibaba and the forty thieves: ("I thought it was a game of cops and robbers.") At the same time the reality of the train with its strident noise, movement, the people around him, is captured in a quick succession of images through which kinetic and visual impulses are set to work:

> The rhythms of the train
> . . .
> The noise of doors voices wheels grinding over the frozen
> tracks
> . . .
> The rustling of women
> And the steam engine's whistle
> And the everlasting sound of wheels whirling madly along in
> their ruts in the sky
> . . .
> And the whole of Europe seen through the windcutter of an
> Express racing ahead at full speed.

Similarly, the story he tells to his companion Jeanne, inviting her to join him on an imaginary journey to dream islands of the Pacific, Mexico, and the North Pole, stands as a foil to the grim reality of this "terrible journey" where "we are the cripples of space." As the train rushes across the Russian plain the poem becomes a real "drunken train after the Drunken Boat" as Jean Cocteau put it.[12] Images, associations of ideas, words without correlatives are tossed out faster and faster in jolting disarray as the mental rhythm accelerates with each turn of the wheels, until the convulsive movement of the transsiberian express becomes the poetic vehicle for the frantic whirling of the universe:

> The world stretches, lengthens and retracts like an
> accordion tormented by a sadistic player
> In the rents of the sky the engines furiously
> Flee
> . . .
> Everything is out of tune
> The "broun roun roun" of the wheels
> Shocks
> Shattering leaps
> . . .
> The train rumbles on revolving plates
> . . .
> And the world, like a clock in the Jewish quarter in Prague,
> turns desperately counterclockwise.

Instead of being carried along the successive narration of a journey the mind is projected into a whirlpool of sensations and thoughts in which past and present become one:

> The railroad is a new geometry
> Syracuse
> Archimedes
> . . .
> Ancient history
> Modern history
> Whirlwinds
> Shipwrecks.

As in Rimbaud's *Drunken Boat* the poet moves back from the immediacy of perception to the recollection of experience, passing from the present tense to a litany-like use of the past "I saw . . . I saw" Once more we find the same binary structure marking the

opposition between the horrors of torture and death in the modern
world and the peace of former ages:

In the pest houses I saw gaping wounds bleeding full blast.
And amputated limbs danced about or took flight in the raucous air.

At the same time his mind is flooded with memories of "the calm
interior, the father's store" of "Moussorgsky and Hugo Wolf
Lieder." Just as Rimbaud yearned for the "black cold puddle" of
European waters, Cendrars ends his journey in Paris:

> Paris
> City of the incomparable Tower of the Rack and the Wheel.

Paris where there is "the most beautiful church in the world" and
"friends who surround /him/ like guardrails."

The multidimensional character of the poem is also strengthened
by the opposition between inner and outer reality, the poet's
consciousness and the flow of impressions, sensations, ideas,
memories, visions which the world thrusts on his sensitivity. The
tale of this epic ride on the TransSiberian, sustained by an apparently inexhaustible creative frenzy, is recurrently interrupted by
the expression of the poet's fear of his limitations. The leitmotiv of
the first stanzas:

> And I was already such a bad poet
> That I could not go to the end

is charged with a darker portent of concern toward the end of the
poem:

> Because I am still a very bad poet
> Because the universe overwhelms me
> . . .
> Because I am not capable of going to the end
> And I am afraid.

In contrast with the perpetual movement of the train's journey, the
poet's spiritual voyage marks reflexive pauses until the actuality of
experience is superseded by the recognition of imagination's win-
ning power:

> When you travel you should close your eyes.

and the poet's acknowledgement of his new creative intent:

> I did not take any notes on my trip.
> . . .
> I have deciphered all the confused texts of the wheels and
> I have assembled the scattered elements of a most violent
> beauty.

Thus in addition to the succession of contrasts in words, images, moods, and tones which capture the diversity of the modern world in its simultaneity *Prose du Transsibérien* also reveals the deeper ontological simultaneity of the subject's relation to the object through the interdependence of the artist's control of his perception and the impact of outer reality on his senses. Cendrars had reached beyond the ambition of Simultaneism. He had found a poetic language attuned to this new era of multiplicity.

His contemporaries did not fail to recognize the unique modernity of the work. As Albert T'Serstevens pointed out, it set a fashion for the following decades and influenced, among others, Paul Morand, Delteil, Mac Orlan, and the Soupault of *Westwego*. After the war the poem was declaimed in several Paris literary salons and Fernand Divoire recalled with emotion the day when the two-meter-long text hung on a wall was read at the "Grenier de Montjoie!": "That day, truly, we had discovered a poet."[13]

III   *An Avowal of Mythopoetic Intent:* Panama ou les Aventures de mes Sept Oncles

If *Prose de Transsibérien* had established Cendrars's reputation as a poet traveller, *Panama* (published only in 1918 but composed in 1913–14) marked a crucial transition which outlined the mythopoetic direction of his future storytelling. This third and last long narrative poem that Cendrars will ever write, is apparently a straightforward discursive tale of adventures and travels which assumes the form of an autobiographical sequence. *Panama* follows through from the poet's early childhood ("I used to play under the table" . . . "I had a fine picture book . . . an English maid"[14]) to his truant days in school ("I was in jail in Marseilles and they took me by force to school"), his return from New York ("I am on my way back from America on the *Volturno* for 35 francs from New York to

Rotterdam") and his Paris life at the time ("I am waiting / I want to be the fifth wheel of the juggernaut / . . . / Nothing and everywhere.") The poet enriches his saga with an ancestry of seven adventurous uncles: a butcher in Galveston, Texas; a gold digger in Alaska and California; a Buddhist in Tahiti who plans to go back to Bombay and dynamite the English settlements; a valet to General Robertson in South Africa during the Boer war; an international chef who served in all the great hotels of the world; an industrialist in South America; an unknown uncle who looks like the poet. But, whether or not these famous uncles were as real as Cendrars later averred in a radio broadcast,[15] the seminal role of imagination is clearly acknowledged throughout the poem.

"There are books on Panama Canal," Cendrars tells us, but this is not the subject of the poem. He makes the point that the Panama financial crash which had ruined his family made him a poet. Why? because while the child was left alone in the chaos of piled up furniture, a letter from one of his uncles came. Just like the picture book of his infancy where:

> the bear the lion the chimpanzee the rattlesnake had taught
> /him/ to read . . .
> those letters with handsome exotic stamps and Rimbaud's verses
> on the label

set him on new fictive paths. The author of *Panama* and the future prose "true stories" will always remain the child for whom a "kitchen stool is an aurochs." The concluding sequences of the poem confirm this openly acknowledged mythopoetic intent. While he mourns the disappearance of good old stories:

> What the hell
> Aren't there any more good yarns
> The lives of Saints
> Das Nachtbuechlein von Schuman
>
> . . .
> Le crocodile de Saint Martin

he knows that the entire universe is contained in his new picture book:

> With the Milky Way around my neck
> And the two hemispheres for goggles

> Full speed ahead.
>
> . . .
>
> Suns moons stars
> Apocalyptic worlds
> All of you have still your parts to play.

Panama also represents a completely new departure in poetic technique. Breaking radically away from the confinement of conventional metrics and traditional poetic structures, Cendrars operates a total modern disjunction of form and reality relying on the sheer force of the word disintegrated and disconnected from emotional charges. The theme of nostalgia echoed by the leitmotiv of the uncle's homesickness is no longer conveyed with the intensity of sadness that pervaded the previous poems. Humor and irony are present everywhere. For instance, the death of one uncle, found with a bullet in his head, is told in the same breath as the news of his wife's remarriage with a jam manufacturer. Snatches of contemporary life carved out from daily papers, publicity slogans, catchwords alternate with exotic images in a manner which at times resembles forms of pop poetry. Often the poet seems to haphazardly jot down whatever comes to his mind as he looks around, or as he leafs through a newspaper. He did not carry his experiment as far as the deliberate search for the incongruous sequence of words—as Dada will a few years later—but he had already taken the first step in that direction. As we know from Albert T'Serstevens, Cendrars confessed that this poem had been inspired by an issue of the review *Tour du Monde*.[16] Many enumerations do look like so many words detached from all emotional content, suggested to the poet by a series of photographs in such a travel magazine. In fact, to promote his new style Cendrars even published the first edition of *Panama* as a travel prospectus with train map tracings separating each section and an advertisement from the Denver Chamber of Commerce inserted in the text, not unlike the insertion of newsreels in Dos Passos's novels.

Just as Cendrars's relationship with his new real and imaginary world is clearly outlined in his avowal of mythopoetic intent his formal break with past poetic structures is no less unequivocally stated. Now that he has embraced the new esthetics of modernity he declares towards the end of the poem:

> This morning is the first day on earth
>
> . . .
>
> Poetry dates from to-day.

IV *Cubist Vision in Poetry:* Dix-Neuf Poèmes Elastiques

Although *Dix-neuf poèmes élastiques* appeared in book form only in 1919, eight of the poems were published five years earlier in *Der Sturm, Montjoie!* and *Soirées de Paris* and all but one ("Construction" was written in February 1919) were conceived at the same time as *Panama.* Often quoted as prototypes of Cubist poetry, these brief terse poetic sketches can be viewed as the most "Modernist" achievement of Cendrars in poetry. Implementing at once his declaration of contemporaneity, Cendrars turned away from his former theme of travel and adventures and focussed on the present, writing what he announced in the postface to the original edition as "occasional poems" inspired by "an encounter, a friendship, a painting, a polemic or a reading." And indeed, to a certain extent, these poems constitute a kind of poetic chronicle of the time. The majority of them are verbal transpositions of the paintings of his friends: Sonia Delaunay's in *"Sur la robe elle a un corps,"* Chagall's in "Portrait" and *"Atelier,"* Roger de la Fresnaye's in *"Natures Mortes,"* Léger's in "Construction." *"Hamac"* is an evocation of Apollinaire and "Mardi Gras" of Canudo whereas *"Crépitements"* lightly satirizes Futurism and *"Fantomas"* is an open attack against Barzun. Others are inspired by moments in his own private life: his attempt at painting in "Journal" and the birth of his son in "Fiat."

The modernity of these compositions does not come, however, from the actuality of their themes but from a kinetic sense of language in which words are projected in their bare physicality in a maximal dissociation between expression and representation. Cendrars still uses the same carefree diary jotting tone and paratactic style as in *Panama,* without punctuation, meter or rhyme, but here he strips language to the utmost, carrying the art of the poetic ellipse a step further, to the extent that a poem becomes a series of apparently unrelated words, acquiring poetic strength from the effect of visual and mental elasticity achieved by the simple act of juxtaposition.

The concept of "elasticity" is not an original feature of Cendrars's poetics. It was one of the keywords of Futurist Manifestoes and, in their quick succession of heterogeneous images telescoped together according to the Cubist principle of fragmentation, the "Elastic Poems" could be seen as an illustration of what Marinetti called "wireless imagination." The very title of the volume may have been

suggested to Cendrars by the painting *"Elasticita"* of the Futurist
Boccioni, and while Cendrars boasted that he was writing stripped
poems without new metaphors or images ("Headlines")—an obvious
hint at Marinetti's statement that "Poetry should be an uninterrupted sequence of new images"[17]—he adopted at times Futurist
imagery such as in "The Head": "The guillotine is the masterpiece of
plastic art."[18] His goal, however, was different. The very dismissal
of Futurism in the poem *"Crépitements"* ("There is no Futurism") is
not only a mischievously open acknowledgment of his lineage (a
very common trick with Cendrars as will be observed later through
the complex intertextual play of his prose works). It is also a genuine
expression of the need to convey the immediacy of contemporary
reality through other means.

Steeped as he was in the climate of Parisian art circles, Cendrars
brought to his poetic experiment of these last prewar years, the
"elasticity" of the four-dimensional range of vision prevalent in
painting, together with the speed of perception of the nascent
cinematographic arts. He knew already, as Fernand Léger would
state it ten years later, that "the eye . . . controls the individual
more than ever."[19] Thus, asking defiantly in *"Aux cinq coins"*:

> Don't I know how to open my eyes
> Poetry is at stake

he flung "the windows of /his/ poetry . . . wide open to the
boulevards" as in *"Contrastes"* and captured lights, colors,
movements, sounds, static and mobile scenes in one single sweep of
a telescopic camera eye:

> Listen to the Limousines violins and the linotypists'
> xylophones
> The inept painter washes with the sky's washcloth
> Everything in splashes of color
> . . .
> In the corner bar
> The workmen in blue shirts are drinking red wine
> Every Saturday chicken in the pot
> They play
> They bet
> From time to time a bandit passes in a car
> Or a child plays with the Arch of Triumph.

Poetry is cleared of any element of thought and the function of the poet becomes the art of selecting the poetic reality present everywhere around him. Driven to the extreme, this practice becomes the art of selecting and arranging words from another text. A newspaper article, a chapter from a book can provide material for this poetry of the immediate daily reality as well as a conventional source of inspiration such as a street scene or any free association of ideas. This is the case of *"Dernière heure,"* a telegram poem carved out of an article of *Paris-Midi,* and "Mee too buggi" inspired, as J. P. Goldenstein demonstrated, by the reading of William Mariner's book on the natives of Tonga island.[20] Yet, as Henry Behar astutely points out, these experiments are not to be equated with those of the Lautréamont-Dada-Surrealism lineage.[21]

Unlike his contemporaries Cendrars does not attempt to give a perturbing disruptive vision of reality. On the contrary, notwithstanding his total adoption of the codes of modernity, he had not abandoned the dream of his youth to "discover . . . cosmic lyricism." (I.S. p. 184)

Thus the "elasticity" sought after in these poems was not only of a visual order, or one based on technical verbal play, it was also a mental and spiritual one. As Cendrars stated later in his articles for *La Rose Rouge,* the Cubist painters only "studied progression through space (the matter of the object), and not progression in depth (the principle of reality)." (vol. 6, p. 41) Accordingly, in order to reach not only the reality of the object but the "principle of reality" of what he will soon call "Profound Today," he practiced a kind of Zenlike discipline of concentration in which the movement of the mind supersedes that of the eye, arresting or accelerating thought at will in a Western form of "Satori." For instance, in the swift transition in *"Contrastes"* from:

> And the hats of women passing by are comets in the evening
> bonfire

to:

> Unity
> there is no more unity

or in the elliptic statement:

> To-day

Change of owner
The Holy Ghost is on sale in the smallest shops.

there is the inner space of a deep meditative look upon the shifting values of the modern world.

In these Modernist experiments par excellence, however close he came to the Cubist and Futurist esthetics, Cendrars remained on a path all his own. Even when his practice of "text-lifting" breaks down all the traditional concepts of the individuality of creation, he never surrenders the subject to the object. Expression may be dissociated from representation. Poetry may be reduced to an art of intertextual montage and yet the conceiving creative subject through his process of selection remains the totalizing force. In this respect, *Dix-neuf poèmes Elastiques* essentially illustrate the author's statement, made in a lecture he delivered in Sao Paulo, that "Poetry reveals the image of the mind that conceived it." (vol. 6, p. 64)

V   *A Poetic Collage:* Documentaires

During the next decade the poetic production of Cendrars dwindled to a trickle. After brief experimentations with typographical innovations in the manner of Apollinaire's *Calligrammes* ("*Sonnet dénaturé*" published in 1923 but composed in 1916), he returned to the form of the *Poèmes Elastiques* with occasional poems like "Shrapnells" written at the beginning of the war in October 1914 and "*Hommage à G. Apollinaire*" composed on the occasion of the poet's death. His most important creation of the time is "*La guerre au Luxembourg*" (October 1916), an ironical evocation of the war as reenacted in children's games in the Luxembourg garden in Paris. In 1917 he wrote "*Au coeur du Monde,*" another mythopoetic construct in which he relates his birth at the "*Hotel des Etrangers,*" 216 Rue Saint Jacques, and discovers for himself an illustrious ancestry (an organ builder, a singer at the "*Chat Noir,*" the mathematician Euler, etc.).

This poem, Cendrars said later, was his farewell to poetry: "In 1917 I had just written a poem which stupefied me. . . . It was so antipoetic! . . . I decided not to publish it and let all modern poetry flounder and manage without me. . . . I put this unpublished poem into a nailed wooden box and placed it in an attic in the countryside. . . . I had decided to wait ten years before I would take it out and publish it." (vol. 13, p. 19) Was it an expression of genuine impatience with the limits of a genre he no longer felt suited to the period, as he time and again stated in letters and interviews, or was it a pose, tinged with a measure of spite that the prewar pioneer of modernity preferred to adopt since he felt that Dada was a "prison" and the nascent Surrealism "brought nothing new"? (vol. 13, p. 33) Cendrars, however, did not wait for ten years. Two years later fragments of *"Le coeur du Monde"* appeared in *Littérature* (ironically enough, the review published by the founders of Surrealism André Breton and Philippe Soupault). Giving the lie to his vow of silence, two more publications were to prove that he had not depleted his stock of poetic innovations.

When *Kodak* (the original title of *Documentaires*) came out in February 1924, it was received as a new chapter of Cendrars's travel diary. It seemed that the poet had decided to focus the telescopic lens of his mind on the world and bring out its diversity in a series of quick verbal snapshots, possibly inaugurating a new genre as he semi-ironically put it, in the foreword to the reprint of the poems ("Document"). With the exception of a brief sequence on elephant hunting in Africa, forty-four out of fifty-five poems describe scenes and people in North America. Divided into chapters by geographical regions ("West," "Far West," "South," "Islands," etc.) the volume does in fact read like a collection of mental photographs taken along a journey. In turn, we see the boat traffic on the Hudson River ("On the Hudson"), a New York multimillionaire in his supermodern office ("Office"), the construction of a wooden bridge ("Trestle Work"), the lush orchards of a Southern California *hacienda* ("Cucumingo"), the wealthy decor of a Southern plantation. The slumbering power of the Mississippi ("River"), the stifling pest-ridden atmosphere of the South ("Vomito Negro") are evoked with as much suggestive strength and accuracy as are the Canadian forests ("Spring" and "Countryside") or the Aleutian islands. Character vignettes such as the Mexican-American dancer in "Dorypha" or the old Indian woman in her trading post ("Squaw Wigwam") are unforgettable pictures.

The novelty of this apparent travelogue is an absence of the narrator's personal commentary and the traditional narrative tone. Objective and self-contained, each poem conveys yet another aspect of the outer and inner reality of the American continent portrayed through a skillful juxtaposition of singled-out elements and the use of a spare and probing idiom manipulated with the precision and

rapidity of optical instruments. The effect of this direct, deliberately
antipoetic, photographic technique disconcerted his first readers
who felt that these "recent poems were to the 'Prose of the
Transsiberian' and to 'Panama' what an album of dead pictures is to
the rapid succession of alive and interwoven images."[22] Nevertheless the authenticity of the travel diary character of the poems was
not questioned, for Cendrars was known for his travels to the New
World (which he was more than prone to multiply at will for the
pleasure of his credulous audience). In 1923, the rumor also ran that
he had been sent to Upper Sudan to shoot a documentary film on
the life of elephants. Thus, for many years, Cendrars was praised for
his art of capturing in vivid sketches the immediacy of the world he
had seen and his new technique was considered as a result of his
recent cinematographic experience.

It is now common knowledge, however, that Cendrars's new mode
was but an extension of his former collage technique inaugurated
in the *Poèmes Elastiques*. What his mental camera had photographed was not actual lands or people, or even the scenery of his
imagination, but the text of a science fiction narrative by a popular
serials' writer, Gustave Le Rouge (1867-1938), and of a travel book
on elephant hunting in the Congo published by Maurice Calmeyn
in 1912. Cendrars had himself revealed part of his subterfuge as
early as 1945 when he announced in his first volume of fictionalized
memoirs, *L'homme foudroyé*:

I was cruel enough to bring a volume of poems to Le Rouge and make him
see . . . a score of original poems I had snipped out of one of his prose
works. (vol. 9, p. 204)

Gustave Le Rouge had fallen into oblivion and it took another two
decades before a French scholar, Francis Lacassin, took Cendrars at
his word and demonstrated that forty-one out of forty-four poems in
Documentaries were carved out of Le Rouge's novel *Le mystérieux
Docteur Cornélius*.[23] As to the source of the other poems, "*Le
Bahr-el-Zeraf*" and "*Chasse à l'éléphant*," Cendrars's help was not
needed. In 1972 T'Serstevens had revealed the poet's reading of
Calmeyn's book and recently Yvette Bozon Scalzitti published a
parallel copy of the two texts.[24] The evidence is blatantly there.
Cendrars did not, in the manner of Lautréamont, only fill his text
with literary reminiscences, nor did he resort to a parody of a fellow
writer's work in the prevalent Surrealist fashion. In both cases

strings of words, complete sentences, at times entire paragraphs are almost faithfully reproduced. The very first page of Le Rouge's novel contains almost word for word the poem "Mushrooming City." Cendrars only shifted from the past to the present tense, dropped a few articles and selected the descriptive elements from Le Rouge's narration of the construction of a new town in the Rockies. Francis Lacassin provides us with an exhaustive account of all the parallel passages. A single instance will suffice:

Around a square where a few beautiful trees were *still standing,* hope of a picturesque public garden, *the steel frames of the thirty storied* houses were starting *to fall in line.* It was a real *forest of metallic beams,* rustling *night and day to the stroke of the hammer,* the creaking noise of *winches* and the *panting* of the *machinery.*[25] (Words not changed by Blaise Cendrars are underlined.)

In Cendrars's poem Le Rouge's prose becomes:

> Around a square where a few beautiful trees are still
> standing a forest of metallic beams rustles night and
> day to the stroke of the hammer
> Winches
> Panting machinery
> The steel frames of the thirty-storied houses start to fall
> into line.[26]

Only the end of the poem differs since Le Rouge's Jorgell city has no name here. Cendrars invigorated the pioneering spirit of the story by wittily adding that the "biggest newspaper in town" opened a competition to baptize the city. On the next page we find that Isadora and her "pigeon blood ruby" in "Amphytrion" is Mr. Jorgell's daughter in the novel. His son Baruch, described by Le Rouge as a Brummel youth inspired the poem "Young Man." The Black Beans' Club in "Club" is also found in Le Rouge. The multimillionaire's office in the poem "Office" is Mr. Jorgell's study. With his usual hyperbolic tendency Cendrars only changed the number of the five telephones to twelve and the two radio sets to five.

A list of such parallels could be endless. Does it mean therefore that we are facing a mere hoax and that, scoffing at the poetic devices of his time, including the Dada custom of collage, Cendrars facetiously published a literary patchwork? We might wonder also whether Cendrars, like a conjurer, blurred his readers' perception in order to prove—in jest—that once a poet has established a myth (in this case the myth of a poet traveller) even science fiction or documentary travel book prose may successfully pass for poetry.

Yet the poetic impact of *Documentaires* is powerful and sure. As Henri Behar[27] noted, with justice, the disclosure of the borrowed subject matter made the pendulum swing from blind admiration for the effect of the picture to disillusioned or cautious comments on the collage technique, whereas both attitudes are largely irrelevant to the seminal emphasis that these poems place on the very notion of poetic discourse. Each poem is a construct, an organic unity in which words are in total congruence with an inner vision of outer reality, in Paul Morand's words an "inscape of outer scapes."[28] Through his verbal tailoring Cendrars imparted to the prose of Le Rouge or Calmeyn a quality of synesthetic perception of the world which is characteristic of all his writings. The poetic "montage" was a true transplant operation: out of a strictly linear prose, he isolated verbal units which took on a poetic dimension only after they had been ordered, contracted and chiselled into his vision. A poem like "Frisco-City" for instance, is taken from Le Rouge's factual account of the shipwreck of a boat called "Frisco City." But in Cendrars the description of the old rusty ship allows for a poetic level of ambiguity and conjures up at the same time an inner sense of the city of San Francisco and its human drama. Even the paratactic inventories of birds, plants, animals convey the exotic beauty of the area whereas in Le Rouge the same language is reduced to its function of providing rational information.

Cendrars said that he performed the "trick" to prove to Le Rouge that he was a poet. The very fact that Le Rouge was not his only source proves that his intent was of a different order. What he was rather demonstrating was his growing concern with the mechanism of expression and the functioning of imagination (a preoccupation already discernable in his early writings and assuming ascending priority in his later prose works). We know from a lecture he delivered in Sao Paulo in 1924 how aware he was of the developing science of linguistics. For him language was for writers, like paints and canvas for a painter, a common property and only the raw material of art. Whether in the unprocessed form of independent signifiers, or already woven into the signifying unit of a previously written text, words are matter and can be given multiple levels of significance, used by a poet as any object became a "ready made" for

Marcel Duchamps, or a beach pebble an elaborate piece of sculpture for George Braque. The hallmark of originality does not lie in the matter used but in the angle in which it is projected by the individual selector. Paradoxically enough, at a time when the Surrealists were experimenting with their technique of "hasard objectif" in order to release the creative powers of the unconscious, Cendrars was demonstrating the essential function of the conscious individual mind, even when deliberately "tinkering" with another writer's text. Modern theoreticians of intertextuality may find in him a forerunner.

VI *Verbal Postcards:* Feuilles de Route

The same year the myth of the world traveller was being consolidated by his readings-inspired *Documentaires,* Cendrars was given the opportunity to apply his talent to real experience. Paris, at that time, was the meeting place of avant-garde artists and writers from all over the world: Americans had been gathering around Gertrude Stein for several years and the Brazilian *"Modernistas"* also had their own "colony" in the French capital. Disgruntled as he was by the dictatorial tyranny which he thought Dada and Surrealism were exerting on poetry, Cendrars was seduced by the youthful enthusiasm of these South American poets and artists. He became a close friend of Oswald de Andrade (one of the most ebullient spokesmen of Modernism and active participant in the 1922 Week of Modern Art in Sao Paulo), and his future wife, the painter Tarsila do Amaral whom he introduced to Fernand Léger and helped to launch an exhibit. He also became acquainted with the Sao Paulo coffee magnate and bibliophile patron of the arts and letters of his city, Paulo Prado. When the latter invited Cendrars to Brazil, at the suggestion of Oswald de Andrade, he grabbed the chance, as he stated later in his collection of stories, *Trop c'est trop,*

only too happy to break away from the chores and the commercialism of the Parisian manifestations in which poetry was confined . . . convinced that to-day's poetry did not belong to an exclusive school but was flourishing all over the world. (vol. 15, pp. 102–103)

Exhilarated by six ocean crossings in the next five years and the dynamism of Brazil, Cendrars postponed once more his decision to renounce poetry, and successively published in 1924, 1926, 1927,

and 1928 the sequence of poems to be later collected in a volume
entitled *Feuilles de Route*.[29]

As the literal translation of the French title implies, these poems
were composed as "travel notes" carrying a step further Cendrars's
desire to do away with literary devices and purge the poetic idiom of
all affectation. The poem "Ocean Letter," which stands out as a kind
of poetic manifesto of this collection, states clearly the demotic
intent of the poet convinced that distinction between prose and
poetry is obsolete and that poetry lives everywhere:

> The ocean letter is not a new poetry genre
> It is a convenient message . . .
> . . .
> The ocean letter has not been invented to write poetry
> But when traveling when doing business when on board when
> sending ocean letters
> One writes poetry.

Later he also described these poems as "postcards /he/ sent or
intended to send to /his/ friends." (vol. 13, p. 26)

The tradition of the postcard style in poetry was not unknown in
this age just discovering the revelatory power and directness of the
camera and looking for ways to impart the same immediacy of
impact to words. In 1902, a French writer Jean Marie Levet had
already published a series of travel poems named "postcards" in *La
Grande France* (April and September issues). Apollinaire, among
others, entitled one of his *Calligrammes* (1913–16) "Postcard" and
another one "Ocean Letter." Even when the term was not used, the
travel-postcard poem was a current fashion of the day before and
after Cendrars's productions (Soupault's *Westwego* [1917–1922],
Morand's *U S A* [1928]). Cendrars's last poetic manner, however,
had nothing in common with the ideogrammatic form practiced by
Apollinaire or the purely pictorial character of other contemporary
writings. Shunning the lyrical exoticism in vogue in the 1920s
(Morand, Supervielle, Claudel, among others), Cendrars presents
few descriptions of South America. With the exception of a handful
of poems such as "Rio de Janeiro," "Sunset," "Bahia," the six poems of
the second section "Sao Paulo" and possibly the series on South American women, his poems are not verbal picture postcards. They are
more informed by his own feelings along the journey than by an
exotic esthetics of diversity.

In a style which defies all critical commentary by its utter candor and simplicity Cendrars reduced his poems to the terse notes of a travel diary. The first section "Formosa," entirely devoted to his crossing from Le Havre to Rio de Janeiro and Santos, chiefly records his sensual and simple delight of being alive in the marvelous freedom of the ocean. We learn about his ecstatic walks at night on deck ("Starred nights"), his preference for sunrises which he is "going to keep for /himself/ alone" ("Sunsets"), his splashes in the upper deck pool ("I swim"), the white suit he bought in Dakar and the cigarettes he carried in his pocket ("White Suit"), his cabin where he "writes all that comes to /his/ mind" ("Cabin No. 6"), his luggage which "weighed 115 pounds without /his/ grey hat" ("Luggage"), his typewriter which "rings at the end of each line and is as fast as jazz" ("Moonlight"). When he evokes people on board we are told more about the fun he himself is having.

I never laughed as much in ten years and laughed during twenty days I laughed myself sick and gained twelve pounds. ("A Fine Evening")

When he chooses to describe a landscape he does it with a startling ironic starkness. The poem "Landscape" for instance states bluntly:

> Red earth
> Blue sky
> Dark green vegetation
> . . .

The third section which centers on his return to France in 1928, after his third visit to Brazil, highlights, as earlier, his own day-to-day adventures on board. His pride at being a versatile conversationalist ("Bad Faith" and "Unmasked Incognito"), the little monkeys who "think they have got /him/ in a cage" ("Hic Haec Hoc" and "Adrienne Lecouvreur and Cocteau") compete in emphasis and importance with descriptions of Bahia, Rio, Pernambucco or his companions on board.

The recurring theme of the poet's open concern with his writings and his writing progress also lends an additional intimacy to these seemingly casual and familiar travel notes. In the poem "Luggage" we are told of all the manuscripts to complete which he carries in his trunk and, on his return voyage, he spends more time typing in his cabin than basking in the tropical sun ("Mornings are mine," "Writing").

> I stay in my cabin
> I suffocate and I write I write . . .

he wrote in the poem "Heat" and characteristically concluded the last section with his shortest so-called poem:

> Why do I write
> Because.

The conception of *Feuilles de route* is carried out on a dual track. On the one hand life on board a transatlantic liner, the boisterous youthfulness of Brazil, the magnificence of the equator are also present in these pages and have the immediate and direct impact of a pure, organically intact impression conveyed in a seemingly artless, extraordinarily accessible form. On the other hand, the author's sensuous happiness, irony, exuberance of being, serenity, yearnings, and an occasional forthright avowal of emotion remain the dominant features. Rather than conveying the exoticism of distant lands, the work engages the reader insofar as it establishes a self. "When I go to Brazil," wrote Dos Passos, "I still see the ascent from Santos to Sao Paulo through Cendrars's eyes." It is indeed his gift of identification to the phenomenon perceived and his keen sense of the instantaneous plenitude of being which gives a poetic vibration to these deliberately apoetic texts, and makes them foreshadowers of the recent trends in confessional sequential poetry.[30]

Many readers have deplored the loss of the lyrical power of *La Prose du Transsibérien*. But at the end of his poetic cycle Cendrars had achieved his goal to write "without ostentation simply, true, as one lives." (vol. 15, p. 24) In its unassuming purity of style this volume offers some of the most memorable poems Cendrars ever wrote, poems which one never forgets such as his "Islands":

> Islands where one will never land
>
> . . .
> Islands of silence
> Islands motionless
> Islands you can't forget and have no name

or poems which continue to resound in the reader's mind such as the popular songlike verses of "You are more beautiful than sky and sea":

When in love you must go away
Leave your wife leave your child
. . .
Leave the woman you love leave the man you love
When in love you must go away.

CHAPTER 4

The Archetypal Figure of the Twenties

ALTHOUGH Cendrars's creative life spanned half a century from 1909 to 1959, to many of his admirers he remained "an archetypal figure of the Twenties."[1] The decade which followed World War One was indeed a most productive one for him. The portrait which Philippe Soupault drew of him as he appeared to him in 1917 is very revealing of the state of mind in which Cendrars returned to the Paris world of arts and letters after his mutilating confrontation with the reality of the war: a blend of disillusionment and creative ebullience which would characterize him throughout his life. Soupault remembered him as: "worried, at times irritated. He wanted to travel and—one thing does not exclude the other— isolate himself." At the same time he also recalled the extraordinary presence of the writer he used to meet regularly at Apollinaire's Wednesdays at the "Café de Flore":

Who was he in 1917? I was truly filled with wonder, dazzled by this poet, a true poet. . . . He was irresistible and in the strongest sense of the term, incredible. He was very sure of himself. . . . He was also lucid . . . his eyes wide open he tried to understand the upheavals that were about to occur.[2]

In spite of his desire to isolate himself, Cendrars was becoming a ubiquitous figure in the artistic and literary world. During the next few years his poems appeared in all avant-garde reviews (*Cabaret Voltaire*, in Zurich, *De Stijl* in Amsterdam, *Valori Plastici* and *Avanscorpeta* in Rome, *Littérature* directed by Breton and Soupault, *Sic* directed by Pierre Albert Birot, *La Revue Européenne* and others). Prose fragments of future works were featured in other French reviews (*Mercure de France, L'Esprit Nouveau, La Caravane, Action*) as well as in foreign publications such as the international review *Broom* of Harold Loeb and even in a local American magazine, *The Plowshare* in Woodstock, New York. Readings of his poems were organized at the "Salle Huygens" and various literary salons such as those of Alfred Mortier, Mrs. d'York, the Baronne d'Oettingen and the Autant-Laras. He was also a familiar in the Café de la Rotonde in Montparnasse, seen in the company of old and new friends he had among painters. This is the time when Picabia, Modigliani, Léger and other less well known artists made several portraits of him. In musical circles, he counted among his friends the composer Eric Satie, and members of the future "Groupe des Six" (Louis Durey, Georges Auric, Darius Milhaud and Arthur Honneger). By 1918 he had already made contact with the film world through his acquaintance with the film director Abel Gance.

The dialogue between Blaise Cendrars and his age is one of reciprocal illumination. The eclecticism of his multiple experiments in every sphere of the avant-garde incarnates vital and powerful forces in France when all the arts seemed aflame with Modernist excitement. In turn, the poet's exuberant, adventurous, and versatile genius was galvanized, by the high voltage atmosphere of variegated creativity and the artistic freedom of the epoch, into successively innovative forms of endeavor.

I *Toward the Abolition of Genres: Poetic Essays or Prose Poems*

Cendrars's first major contribution to the spirit of the 1920s preceded the famous decade. Dissatisfied as he was with the current trends in poetry, he found a mode of writing more congenial to his all-encompassing awareness of modern sensibilities. The two short texts he published in 1917 and 1918, *Profond Aujourd'hui* and *J'ai tué*, announced on the cover page of the first editions simply as "prose," may be considered prose poems in the tradition of Rimbaud's *Illuminations*. On the other hand, they prefigure the reduction of the distinction between prose and poetry operated in the contemporary "discourse" of the antinovels or the most recent "new new" French novels.

In one uninterrupted paragraph, four pages long, *Profound Today* capsulizes the antinomian character of the age with its dissociation of sensibilities and yet its totalizing consciousness. To capture the pulse and beat of the modern world Cendrars developed a kind of psychedelic style in which thought proceeds by quantum leaps. Regular syntax, always in the present tense, alternates with incomplete sentences or single words hurled one after the other—units the mind registers as if propelled by a dynamo. Noting the "absolute

modernity" of Cendrars's new manner in his review of this text in
Nord Sud, Reverdy wittily warned the reader that from now on we
"must notice that our brain is a dynamo fitted to a type-writer."[3]
This jerky, deliberately mechanized concentrated prose was a perfect vehicle to express the psychic tension of the modern era
projected by Cendrars. On one hand this near Surrealistic essay
reads like an ecstatic hymn to the "Prodigious to-day" in which

Cosmogonies live again in the trademarks. . . . Matter is as well trained as
the stallion of an Indian chief. . . . Everything is sensitized . . . that tin-can
is a poem of ingenuousness. . . . Products from the five parts of the world
are featured in the same plate on the same dress. . . . All is artificial and
quite real. (vol. 6, p. 3–4)

There is a certain cockiness in the way the author pretends to
believe he has found the cipher key to the modern world. On the
other hand there is simultaneously an implied indictment of
modernity which foreshadows a postModern awareness. The

labyrinth of department stores where you give up your entity to become
everyone" (p. 4)

adumbrates Le Clezio's satire of the megamarkets in *Les Géants*.
The industrialization of tourism which turns individuals into herded
cattle is also caricatured, a theme recently echoed in Didier De-
coin's novel *Trois milliards de voyages*. Together with the mes-
merizing power of this multidimensional age, the general loss of
identity of the human being atomized in the kaleidoscopic reality
of things is sensed throughout the text.

As will be frequently observed in the following chapters, the
surge of optimistic confidence in this technological age is tempered
by strains of pessimistic doubt. This "Gospel of modern civilization," as Jean-Claude Lovey described *Profond Aujourd'hui*, also
raises the question which underlies all the future works: "Where is
Man?"

The same question is again implied in *J'ai tué* published the
following year. A brief narrative of a military offensive, it finally
projects with scathing irony the dissolution of man's integrity in the
man-made machinery of war. At first the war atmosphere is evoked
in a quick percussive prose even more stripped of stylistic effects
than that of *Profond Aujourd'hui*. In lapidary verbal units which
anticipate Robbe-Grillet's scientific objectivism, movements,

sounds, men, and things are registered impassively without a trace of ethical implication. The desolation of an occupied deserted town, for instance, is suggested by a factual notation: "A yellow novel on the sidewalk, a wash-basin, a bottle of cologne." (p. 7) A bombing raid is recorded in brief notations such as:

Everything bursts, cracks, thunders, all at the same time. General conflagration. A thousand detonations. Fires, blazing masses, explosions. . . . Devastated countryside. Frozen grass. Dead lands. Sickly stones. (p. 9)

But after that impersonally relentless artillery charge of words the text gives way to the author's sense of the incongruity of it all. Summoning to his mind centuries of civilization's achievements, he concludes on a note of exaltation, edging on sarcasm and despair as he relives a hand-to-hand fight in which modern weaponry is bested by the primitive knife:

And here I am to-day with a knife in hand. . . . "Long live Humankind." . . . I gave the first stab. I have got the sense of reality, I, a poet. I acted. I killed. As a man who wants to live. (p. 12)

J'ai tué, is closer in theme and style to the narrative mode of a short story than *Profond Aujourd'hui*. In both texts a concentration of vision and thought, the blend of personal narrative and abstract projection of the "new spirit" make a poetic impact seldom as successfully achieved. Cendrars had developed a literary medium which convincingly reflects the artistic freedom of the age.

Another foray into prose form experimentation, combined the writer's qualities of factual narration and imaginative poetic vision in a short work which also eludes classification.

The circumstances of the composition of *L'Eubage* could invite the reader to consider this narration of an interplanetary journey as a piece of "*littérature alimentaire*," in which the author enjoyed reinforcing his legendary status of world roamer with a chapter on space travel. Cendrars had been asked for an unpublished manuscript by Jacques Doucet, the wealthy Parisian *couturier* who became a well-known patron of the arts and letters in the first decades of the century. Their correspondence, between May 1917 and January 1918, shows that the writer sent the text in chapter installments against monthly payments, taking care all the while to shroud the command performance in the myth of a journey he might have personally undertaken.

What I send you is the pure and simple account of the journey I made in the suprastellar mountains, an unexplored area which is like the hinterland of the sky.

He wrote this to Jacques Doucet on May 3, 1917 in an introductory letter to his first pages, presenting himself as an "eternal exile."[4] Later in his life, Cendrars assumed a pose of indifference towards that work, dismissing it as a mere literary exercise, "a little book that does not have much to it" ("Un petit livre de rien du tout"), a "scientific document" which became "outdated." (vol. 13, pp. 92, 91) The very fact, however, that he chose to reproduce the quoted part of his letter on the front page of the publication, ending it with the more dramatic formula, "The Eubage in exile" (vol. 2, p. 37), confirms the consistency of his mythmaking intent, and indicates the scope of his ambition. At the time of its publication in 1926, the original title, "At the Antipodes of Unity" (kept as a subtitle), had become L'Eubage, a most revealing choice since an eubage is an ancient Gallic priest who specialized in astronomy and divination.

Divided into twelve chapters, each meant originally to correspond to a sign of the Zodiac, but later identified by the name of the months, the story seems at first to be a cross section between science fiction works in the Jules Verne style or La guerre des Vampires of Gustave Le Rouge and a philosophical tale in the manner of Cyrano de Bergerac.[5] There is less scientific precision, however, than in regular science fiction works and soon the symbolic imagination of the poet takes over:

I believe we have travelled in an eye and I had collected glances like a bunch of flowers. The wheat blades of the brain (p. 54)

the narrator said at the end of the sixth chapter, underscoring the interiorization process of the adventure. The function of unreality rules out the function of reality.

The diaries published in Inédits Secrets indicate the early acquaintance (1906) of Cendrars with Camille Flammarion's L'Astronomie populaire and his general fascination with esoteric branches of knowledge. In her analysis of this "cosmodrama" as she has labelled it, Jacqueline Chadourne shows that Cendrars's lineage in this work is to be found less in science fiction than in the time honored tradition of cosmogonic literature ranging from Plato to Novalis, through Jean Paul Richter and Edgar Allan Poe. What the visionary astronaut (the *eubage*) sees once he has broken his moorings from Earth, are the archetypal figures which structure our dreams. The "Eel" or "Snake of the sky," the "Sponge of darkness" which "as a brain in a skull . . . molds itself in the primary form" (p. 42), the gigantic butterfly which takes the space ship in tow, at times lifting it "in the refulgence of his bright head" at times burying it in "the darkness of its belly" (p. 47), reveal more about the inner landscape of the mind than the topography of outer space. In fact, Cendrars's imaginary journey into space assumes the tone of a metaphysical voyage to the far reaches of the mind which probes into the limitations of man's grasp of the laws of the universe:

How could that serous discharge of the brain, which goes by the name of scientific reasoning, take the universe apart or define a blade of grass since science is ignorant of the most primary processes of the universe? (p. 48)

asks the *eubage* wondering whether his enterprise is not an imposture.

Such epistemological querying points to the fundamental metaphysical anguish of the writer. Under the guise of a purely imaginary fantasy, "like a poet who speaks or pretends to speak nonsense" (p. 49), Cendrars's odyssey through space is in the tradition of analogical thought developed by the alchemists. The hermetic undertones become clear in the last chapter when, just before the final explosion which will bring him back to earth, the last vision the *eubage* (i.e. the poet) has before fainting is that of a "zig zag in the form of a question mark." (p. 68)

In line with his frequent declarations of demotic intent as a poet, *L'Eubage* could be read as a farewell to the dreams of the *Poètes Maudits*, a temporary foray into the unreachable infinite before a final return to reality. Seen in relation to the earlier poet-Christ's agony in *Moganni Nameh*, the future quest for the "universal rhythm" of Moravagine and the esoteric meaning of the study of levitation in *Lotissement du Ciel* (see chapters 5 and 7), this cosmogonic journey appears as a keystone to Cendrars's total body of work. An appendix to the fifth chapter of this text, on the history and the origin of the idea of perpetual motion, reinforces this point of view. Cendrars's insistence on the spiritual significance of the quest for "self motive power" and the recurrence of the theme in later works proves that he was envisaging the functioning of creative imagination as a manifestation of the desire to transcend the spatial and temporal limitations of the mind.[6] *L'Eubage,* paradoxically, may indeed be the only true autobiographical piece Cendrars ever wrote, a glimpse into a spiritual inner life which otherwise will always be carefully protected behind the barricade of the "true stories" of a partly fictive outer life.

II   *A New Medium: the Cinema*

As for most of his contemporaries, literature alone could not contain Cendrars's inexhaustible creative vitality. After the First World War, when Charlie Chaplin's films, the Mack Sennett Keystones, the Rio Jim Westerns of William S. Hart flooded the Paris movie theaters, enthusiasm for the emerging film arts spread like a tidal wave. Apollinaire had written several essays and poems on cinema and in 1917 had composed a *"cine-drama" La Bréhatine* which remained unpublished. By 1917–18 the "cinematograph," to use the term of the time, had inspired Max Jacob, Reverdy, Philippe Soupault, Aragon, among many others.[7]

Always open to any totalizing form of artistic expression, Cendrars was naturally affected by the general craze. The fragments of *L'A B C du cinéma* (1926) which he published in various reviews in 1919 testify to his enthusiasm for the seventh art, which he eulogized at times, to delirious heights. In his typical blending of scholarly erudition and fantasy he proclaimed with prophetic intensity that the cinematographic arts were to become the language of a race of new human beings, the Gospel of tomorrow, the fourth revolution after the three previous ones of the importation of the Phoenician alphabet by Cadmus to Greece, the discovery of printing and the invention of the radio. (vol. 6, pp. 20–24)

What is distinctive about Cendrars's attraction to that world is that, beyond the usual literature/cinema relationship, his interest in motion picture art was based on active experience. There is no proof, so far, of his association with the Pathé Motion Picture Company for which he boasted to have made several documentaries and short reels before he met the avant-garde film director Abel Gance. But in 1918 he did assist Gance in the shooting of the war film *J'accuse.* Invited as a stand-in character to figure a corpse with his amputated arm daubed with hemoglobin, he ended up by being everything on the set from errand boy to assistant cameraman. It is at that time that he started to work for Abel Gance on the script of a film, *Les Atlantes,* which was never to be made.[8] In the next Abel

Gance production, the technically innovative *La Roue* which became a classic of film history, he participated as assistant director in the shooting of scenes in St. Gervais, Nice, and Rome (1921–22). According to Abel Gance, however, Cendrars, lacking professional knowledge of filmmaking technicalities, was primarily entrusted with the responsibility of a production manager.[9] Nevertheless, the famous train scene bears Cendrars's unmistakable stamp and so does the general spirit of *La Roue* which Léger described as "the first French film which managed to individualize the object and the fragment of the object"[10]—a typically Cendrarian quality.

His work with Abel Gance in Rome led to a contract with the Rinascimento Studios for which he was to direct a film entitled *La Vénus Noire* starring the Indian dancer Dourga. Dourga's accident, Mussolini's push on Rome, and probably Cendrars's lack of experience all combined to bring this experiment to an end in 1922.[11] What issued from this experience is an exceedingly baroque scenario published the same year as *La perle fiévreuse*. Presented as a shooting script cut up in eight hundred and fifty sections, it appears to be a satirical "potpourri" of contemporary melodrama. Various personalities—Cendrars's own creations, legendary characters such as Fantomas, Nick Carter, Arsene Lupin, Rouletabille, and real people—to name Conan Doyle and Gustave Le Rouge—thronged through a medley of variegated plots. The script is interesting as evidence of the familiarity the writer had acquired with the technicalities of cinematographic language.

The most original creation which Cendrars's flirtation with film arts inspired is *La fin du monde filmée par l'Ange Notre Dame*, conceived as early as 1916 before his exposure to the studios (as a prepublication in the review *La Caravane* indicates).[12] In the 1919 volume of *"Les Editions de la Sirène"* this unclassifiable text was presented as a "novel." Such genre identification was probably the whimsical result of Cendrars's disappointment when what he intended as a film did not find an outlet in the motion picture world, for this "novel-scenario" is definitely composed as a film script. Its poetic language does not reveal the technical knowledge acquired during the Rome experience, but its fifty-five terse paragraphs grouped in seven sequences show an obvious awareness of current film techniques.

The story reads like an unabashed caricature of American melodramas in vogue and the Keystones comedy chases. God our Father, featured as a stereotypical American businessman, sits in his

American office on earth, smoking cigars and making furious tele-
phone calls to his store department heads (the Pope, the Great
Rabbin, the Great Lama, etc.). From Interlaken he leaves for the
planet Mars on an interplanetary train propelled by "giant
dynamos." Once in Mars-city, the "Barnum of religions," he views
the weekly circus parade headed by all the founders of religions
from Krishna to Jesus, followed by "evil deities" in a cage, with
Charlot (Charlie Chaplin) on stilts bringing up the rear in the group
of the "quacks." The Martians, a fragile and peaceful people, who
live in soap bubbles are frightened by the cruelty and the vulgarity
of that display and send their police to break up the procession. God
escapes to the desert and ends up at the "Grand Hotel" in Adventurers' City where, fascinated by the grandiose spectacle of war on
earth, he plans to open a movie house in which he will show the
"best war films." His factotum, Menelik, reminds him that the
Martians are pacifists and suggests He carry out the prophesies of
the Old Testament. The trumpet-blowing angel of Notre Dame in
Paris is sent a message and starts shooting a film from the top of the
cathedral. After a series of panoramic views of the city, the camera
focusses on the cathedral and, when the angel blows his trumpet,
the whole world tumbles to its apocalyptic end. Then an "accelerated and slow motion" shows the re-creation of the world with all
the exotic species of plants and wild animal life, until a fuse is blown
in the camera and the film spins backward at full speed reversing the
action in fast motion.

In this humorous fantasy, some of Cendrars's inventions anticipate the films of Calvacanti and René Clair. A parallel has even been
made between the episode of the Martians in their soap bubbles and
the last scene of *2001: A Space Odyssey*. [13] Had Cendrars found a
producer at the time, it would have been a history making film, but
it would have required all the resources of presentday film technology to do justice to Cendrars's imagination.

Yet, in spite of all his intuition of the potential of cinematographic arts, Cendrars remained primarily a poet. Soon after his
association with the Rinascimento Studios the love affair with the
motion picture world ended in a "divorce due to temperamental
incompatibility" as Cendrars worded it in his interviews with
Michel Manoll. (vol. 13, p. 134) Nonetheless, the immense
technological and artistic potential of the film industry made a
permanent impression on the writer. He would return, again and
again, to his own brief but intense and exciting contact with it,

fictively transformed in his literary creations. *La Fin du Monde* was characteristically given mythic status when it became a creation of his hero Moravagine. His next main protagonist, Dan Yack, realizes Cendrars's ambition as a film producer. A short story *"Etc. . . etc. . . Un film 100% brésilien"* is the epic account of a grandiose and purely imaginary plan for a large-scale film production in Brazil.[14] Cendrars's fascination for the film arts will haunt his future works and at times bear a direct influence upon their narrative style or structure.

III   *Art Criticism*

Another interest which Cendrars shared with his contemporaries was art criticism. As he put it in a 1951 interview with André Parinaud, those were the days when every painter

went hand in hand with a poet. Braque with Reverdy; Picasso with Max Jacob; I with Delaunay, Chagall, Léger; Apollinaire with the School of Paris.[15]

We have already noted that most of the major artists of the period were among his closest friends. Almost every first edition is enhanced by a portrait of Cendrars or illustrations by such leading artists as Modigliani, Picabia, Léger, the Brazilian painter Tarsila and also Csaky, Jean Hecht, Moise Kisling, Angel Zarraga. At one time he was Modigliani's constant companion in Paris and Nice. Picabia became a neighbor in Le Tremblay sur Mauldre, Cendrars's *"pied à terre"* near Paris until it was ransacked during the Second World War. Braque was still a frequent guest of his in Aix-en-Provence in the 1940s. In 1954, in a dialogue recorded with Fernand Léger, and the gallery owner, Louis Carré, for the opening of a Léger exhibit, Cendrars evoked his daily *apéritifs* with Léger during the pre World War I years. (vol. 14, p. 303)

Cendrars's interest in art was not a mere consequence of all these encounters. Several traces of it can be found in his early diaries and soon after his arrival in Paris, in 1912, he wrote an article on The *"Douanier Rousseau,"* published in the January, 1913 issue of the German Review *Der Sturm.* He had also translated into German Apollinaire's *Méditations Esthétiques* for the same review. In March 1913 Apollinaire used Cendrars as a ghost writer for his art chronicle in *Les Indépendants.* Cendrars's personality was so little suited to that type of assignment that the experience did not last longer than a week. He did not find a forum for his own theories until May 1919 when Maurice Magre offered him a section of his own in *La Rose Rouge*, where he published the series of articles entitled *"Modernités."* (vol. 6, pp. 36–51)

Taking his familiar stance of the prophet of modernity, he opened fire in the very first issue with an attack against Cubism in which he predicted the disintegration of the "anonymous collective cube" in favor of a more personal sensuous art of color, of a "new interpretation of man" in line with the "new beauty" apprehended by the poets. In the following articles he illustrated his theory with examples of three "anti-theoreticians of the group," Picasso, Braque, Léger, owing to whom the "cubist experience was not entirely negative," also an analysis of Leopold Survage's study on the circular movement of colors and a text on Delaunay and the simultaneous contrast. In spite of the extraordinary pertinence of some of his comments, on Picasso or Léger, for instance, Cendrars's approach lacked precision and achieved originality only when the poet superseded the historian of art. His collaboration with the *Rose Rouge* was to be shortlived, since it came to an end within three months in July 1919.

Was he truly disappointed by the modern painters who, instead of bringing about the renewal he dreamt of, were turned into "bourgeois" moneymakers with the booming industry of art collecting and dealing, as he frequently stated later in various interviews? Or was he simply too doggedly independent to submit to the routine of weekly assignments? Whatever the true reasons for this second "divorce" might have been, Cendrars's talents were already engaged on another front: the publishing business.

IV *Publishing Experiments*

In the 1920s the publishing business still flourished as an independent private enterprise and the tradition of innovative experimental publications was very much alive. An omnivorous reader like Cendrars with his explorer's flair for rare and unknown texts would naturally be attracted by any opportunity for productive and lucrative action which he thought the field could offer. In 1918, the banker Paul Laffitte invited Cendrars to become an associate literary director in his publishing house of "Les Editions de la Sirène." If Cendrars's statement in the "Pro Domo" of *La fin du Monde* (2nd

ed.) were to be taken seriously, within a year he would have
launched a gigantic program of publications: collections of Alexan-
drian and Byzantian novels, music and art notebooks, anthologies of
modern poets, reprints of Villon, Nerval, Lautréamont, unpublished material of Mallarmé and Radiguet, countless numbers of
other projects amounting to a total of two hundred and twenty-one
volumes. It is evident that a large margin must be allowed for the
hyperbolic tendency of the publicity minded myth-maker. The fact
remains, however, that this function was not a mere bread-winning
interlude. It was befitting to the library haunting side of Cendrars,
already recognized by Apollinaire a few years earlier in *Le Flâneur
des deux rives*. The 1919 catalogue of La Sirène is an interesting
example of Cendrars's influence: such titles as Baudelaire's *La
Fanfarlo* and *Le Coeur mis à nu*, a volume of Villon's poems, and *Le
Bestiaire* by Apollinaire clearly reflected his taste. One of the most
important productions of La Sirène for which Cendrars may also be
credited is the publication of *Memoires du Chevalier de Seingalt*,
Casanova's memoirs of which at least one volume came out in 1924.
Cendrars, however, had not even waited long enough to carry out
this favorite project of his. By 1921 he had already abandoned the
whole enterprise when his passion for filmmaking took over and sent
him to Rome.

V   *Cendrars, Editor of African Tales*

Another manifestation of Cendrars's versatility and sensitivity to
the tastes of the period is the publication in 1921 of his anthology of
African tales *Anthologie nègre* which he prepared while he was
working at "La Sirène."

The influence of African art in France since the discovery of masks
by the painters Vlaminck and Derain was already widespread. The
famous *Demoiselles d'Avignon* of Picasso was but one of the popular
examples. But, in spite of the studies of the German ethnologist Leo
Frobenius which stressed the wealth and originality of oral African
literature as early as 1910, the African creative genius was known to
the French primarily through its masks and dances. Cendrars's
compilation of missionaries' or explorers' accounts of ancient African
tales was therefore received as a significant event which imposed
upon the public a textual presence of African thought. As the poet
and ethnologist Michel Leiris stated: "More than a book it is an act."
(vol. 3, p. XVI)

Cendrars, however, was not as much of an innovator in this domain as it was alleged at the time. Martin Steins pointed out in a recent monograph that such anthologies had appeared in France as early as 1903[16] and *L'anthologie nègre* "stands as a supporting pillar of the cult of the Cendrarian myth."[17] Cendrars's timing, nevertheless, was perfect. Published in the same year as the Pan African Congress held in Paris, London, and Brussels, Cendrars's African anthology was indeed an act of double significance in relation to Cendrars's own evolution at the time. Presented by the author as an illustration of his intellectual conviction that:

the study of the languages and literatures of primitive races is one of the most essential branches of knowledge for the historian of the human mind, (vol. 3, p. 4)

it also reflected Cendrars's personal attraction to ancient and primitive myths and fables. He found in them the raw instantaneous quality of life, the sense of magic, the intensity of feelings, the crude humor which would pervade some of his future writings. There is such a congruence between the writer's own storytelling style and his selection of African tales that it becomes difficult to draw the line between erudition and imagination.[18]

Cendrars was going to exploit this popular vein once more towards the end of the decade when the fashion of African lore had reached an even wider public. According to the author's statement in the radio interviews with Michel Manoll, he was planning to bring out two additional volumes of African folklore made up of material found at the British Museum and oral sources collected in Brazil. It was assumed therefore that two small brochures published in 1928 and 1930, *Petits Contes nègres pour les enfants des Blancs* and *Comment les Blancs sont d'anciens Noirs* represented a partial achievement of the original project. Owing to Martin Steins's research it is now known that far from resulting from Cendrars's personal knowledge, these volumes are merely an adaptation of tales collected by Father H. Trilles, a nineteenth-century missionary.[19]

This African interlude in Cendrars's production may thus be looked upon as a mere example of literary opportunism. To a certain extent, it is another instance of the author's attempt to escape from the constraints of Parisian literary trends as were his previous experiments in film arts, the ballet, and art criticism. On the other hand, viewed in parallel with his future prose work it rather appears to be a first illustration of Cendrars's art of storytelling as an art of re-creation.[20]

VI *Cendrars and the "Ballets Suédois"*

L'anthologie nègre was to provide one more outlet for Cendrars's versatile genius. It gave him an entry into another dynamic form of the arts at the time: the ballet world. For more than a decade already Diaghilev's *"Ballets Russes"* had aroused the interest of the Paris avant-garde. By the 1920s several companies attempted to rival them in modernity and called upon the leading artists. Thus Cendrars was asked to adapt one of his African tales for Rolf de Maré's and Jean Borlin's *"Ballets Suédois."* It is not difficult to imagine the enthusiasm with which Cendrars must have collaborated with the composer Darius Milhaud and Fernand Léger, who was in charge of stage scenery and costumes, for the realization of this ultra modern ballet entitled *La Création du Monde*. The première on October 25, 1923 at the "Théatre des Champs Elysées" was somewhat of an epoch making event.

Cendrars had long been interested in music, as his 1913 study on Russian composers shows (*Inédits Secrets*, pp. 323–51). Later in his life he would write opera librettos which have remained unpublished. On the wave of success of *La Création du Monde* he had many other projects for the *"Ballets Suédois,"* but his departure to Brazil in 1924 brought them to an end. One of his librettos entitled *Après-diner*[21] was apparently the source of Eric Satie's ballet *Relaches*. According to James Harding,[22] Cendrars's original idea was radically transformed by Picabia.

It may seem that restlessness or wanderlust are to be credited for the transient character of these successive activities. Well suited as the idea is to the image of the legendary Cendrars, this was not, however, the sole factor, for his gifts at that time were seeking, like water, their true level. He was already absorbed in a creative effort of far greater scope: three of the five novels he published year after year in the second half of the decade were to give birth to the two most powerful characters he will ever conceive: Moravagine and Dan Yack.

CHAPTER 5

The Novel of Adventure and the Adventure of the Novel

AT a time when the traditional novel was being exposed to virulent attacks by André Breton who considered "the generous supply of novels" the result of a general stultification of the mind and reproached each novelist for adding "his personal little 'observation' to the whole,"[1] Cendrars felt that the novel alone would provide a space of sufficient magnitude for his vision and the projection of the "deep transformation of to-day's man." In a notice published in *Tous les livres* in April 1929, he asserted that the formula of the novel alone could develop the "active character" and the "movement" of contemporary events and people. He concluded with the confident statement that "For some five years, the French novel in the world helps to set up the new regime of human personality." (vol. 6, p. 35)

Undoubtedly the five-year period refers to his own production since 1925. His four novels, *L'Or*, *Moravagine*, *Dan Yack* and *Rhum*, in spite of the apparent variety of form and themes, are unified by an underlying phenomenological preoccupation with the new shifting identity of man in an age of excess, violence, erotic distortions, and psychic aberrations. Whether he presents historical figures like Sutter and Galmot in *L'Or* and *Rhum*, or semi-autobiographical phantasms like Moravagine and Dan Yack, a recurring pattern defines his characters. Cendrars, however, was not a writer who could attach himself to a particular genre any more than he could settle into a single literary movement. Beyond the thematic significance of the heroes a study of these four works will delineate a creative cycle in which the myth of Cendrars as an author of adventure stories is replaced by the more modern image of an adventurer in fictional forms.

76

I   L'or [Sutter's gold]: *A Parable of Modern Greed
or the Epic of a Disappearing Race of Adventurers*

According to the correspondence published in *Inédits Secrets*
Cendrars was introduced to the legendary figure of Johann August
Sutter as early as 1912 by his friend, the Swiss sculptor August
Sutter, a grandson of this last great colonial pioneer of America. The
Swiss Cendrarian scholar, Hugues Richard, has recently proved,
however, that Cendrars's knowledge of General Sutter's story can
be traced back to his early childhood when he and his brother used
to read pages of a local Swiss almanac, *Le messager boiteux,* used as
toilet paper in their family home! In the same essay, Hugues
Richard reveals the direct source of Cendrars's inspiration: a
monograph published in 1868 by Martin Birmann, a church minis-
ter and State Counsellor under whose protection Sutter's children
were placed after Sutter's escape to California.[2]

However multiple Cendrars's sources may be, the choice of the
Swiss adventurer as a topic for a first novel is not surprising. With
his acute sense of the absurd the future author of *Eloge de la vie
dangereuse* would be drawn to the tragic irony of a destiny shattered
by ill fortune in the guise of good luck. "A man ruined by the
discovery of gold! Magnificent, magnificent, magnificent!" reads the
postscript to a letter to his friend, the sculptor Sutter. (I.S. p. 265)
However, it was only many years later, after his first visit to Brazil,
that within six weeks he wrote the story of this quixotic hero of the
last frontier years and victim of the Gold Rush. One may wonder
whether this acquaintance with the Brazilian open lands already
booming with the frenzy of modern industrial growth did not serve
as a catalytic agent to stir his interest in those pioneering days of the
conquest of California, when untrammelled individualism was
making its last ditch stand before the encroachment of faceless
modern society.

The history of the Swiss fugitive provided Cendrars with all his
favorite themes. The actual Sutter was a man who bought his
passage to New York with a falsified letter of credit, resorted to
forgery, swindles, robbery, fabulations of all kinds along his Westward trek and via the Sandwich Islands and Sitka made it to the bay
of San Francisco. He finally wangled a land grant and subsidies from
the Mexican governor in Monterey, all the while craftily courting
the Indians. There was no lack of adventure, wars, violence,
dangerous living, land and sea travels, exotic characters of the type

that will abound in Cendrars's later short stories. Yet, in this first narrative he showed extraordinary restraint in the use of this material. What emerges is an allegorical parable rather than a standard historical novel or tale of adventure.

In an unusually spare and classic manner—up until Sutter's settlement in California—Cendrars relates the essential facts of Sutter's odyssey: a brief account of his family background, his fruitless attempt to obtain a passport legally in the little Swiss village of Runenberg, his escape to France through the forests, the arrival in New York, his first farming experiment in Missouri, various stages of his journey through Fort Independence, Fort Boise, and Fort Vancouver, negotiations in Honolulu for the exportation of Kanakas to the empire he plans to build in California and his landing from a Russian schooner on the beach of the future San Francisco. Dates, names, and figures are faithfully recorded with a journalist's precision and major events are suggested with the conciseness of a film scenario. The great lover of ocean crossings curbed his poetic impulse to the utmost. Sutter's passage to New York, for instance, is only noted with a brief entry:

> The Harbor
> New York's harbor
> 1834. (vol. 2, p. 143)

The second more exotic sea voyage from Vancouver to the Sandwich Islands is recorded with the dry accuracy of a logbook and the other two journeys from Honolulu to Sitka and down the Pacific Coast are merely mentioned. Similarly, the excitement, the risks, dangerous shady dealings involved in any pioneering trek Westwards are soberly understated. The description of the departure for Fort Independence in June 1838 is crisp and brief:

> The caravans are getting ready. A crazy confusion of animals and goods. People call at each other in all languages. Busy Germans, Frenchmen, Englishmen, Spaniards, Indians, Negroes jostle each other. People travel on horseback, in carts, in long covered wagon trains drawn by 12 pairs of oxen. Some alone, others with a large company. (vol. 2, p. 152)

The progression of the narrative, relentlessly kept to a fast straightforward pace, does not allow the reader or the hero even time for a reflective pause. The various stages of Sutter's progress are merely punctuated at the end of each section with telegraphic comments such as: "he is possessed" (p. 149), "He is ready." (p. 152), "Sutter remains alone" (p. 154), "Sutter is in a hurry" (p. 160), "That's what Sutter comes to conquer" (p. 164), "And he steps in" (p. 167). Allowing free scope to the imagination of the reader, Cendrars skillfully escaped the tedious clutter of factual data found in faithful historical accounts or travelogues.

The poetic liberties that Cendrars took with the actual facts of Sutter's life in the remaining chapters, from his settling down in Sacramento Valley to his final spiritual and financial ruin after the discovery of gold on his lands, illustrate a mythopoetic intent. Although the real Sutter, as we know him from Zollinger's detailed and earnest biography,[3] was a man after Cendrars's own heart with his bemusing double personality—half hero, half rascal, cynical fabulist and debonair idealist, ruthless imperialist and naive philanthropist—the contradictions of his character are completely obliterated. Nor is any mention made of the miscellaneous intricate operations in the acquisition of his lands and the development of his fabulous estate. Pressing on steadily to the image he wanted to build, Cendrars discarded pertinent documentation to focus on the tragic destiny of a man ruined by gold. Upon this vision rests the burden of the novel.

From the dramatic seventh chapter which capsulizes the surging Gold Rush in ten lines the narrative takes on the tone of an ancient Christian parable. Deliberately ignoring the fact that Sutter was himself contaminated by the Gold Rush fever, that his properties were mortgaged before the invasion of his lands by myriad squatters, that he was also ruined by a feud with his oldest son and his own prodigality, Cendrars lends Sutter the stature of a hero in a Greek tragedy, victim of fate or God's wrath. Gold becomes an allegory. It is an evil force which breaks up the peace of the hardworking rural community:

> It is peace. No. No. No. No. No. No. No. No. No: it's GOLD.
> It's Gold
> The Rush
> The Gold Rush swooping over the world. (p. 181)

Like a modern Sisyphus, Sutter braves ill fortune and three times rebuilds his devastated domain until the infuriated mob in a kind of frenzy sets fire to his last refuge and his spirit is crushed by the spectacle of the apocalyptic scene of his slaughtered herds, ransacked crops, and the bodies of his last faithful farm hands hanging in the trees. To add pathos to his imaginative account Cendrars has Sutter's wife die melodramatically on the steps of her husband's dwelling upon her arrival from Europe. (She actually survived Sutter by a year.) Another fictive episode concerns Sutter's oldest son. According to Cendrars he became a lawyer, successfully handled his father's suits against the state until the daimon of popular revenge set fire to his offices and destroyed all the documents in support of his father's case. The final days of the real Sutter, quietly living, and again in style, with his wife in Lititz, Pennsylvania, as Zollinger established it, did not suit Cendrars's tragic imagination. He completed his mythic construct by transforming his hero into a religious visionary wandering about in total destitution with the Apocalypse in his pocket.

His version of General Sutter's death is also most characteristic of his art of drawing a myth out of reality. Sutter actually died in a hotel room in Washington, D.C., two days after he had been informed that Congress had adjourned for the year before a bill in his favor on the agenda was discussed. Cendrars staged the scene with the stark effectiveness of Greek tragedy: once more the victim of human mischief, Sutter dies from shock on the steps of the Capitol when a young boy runs down the steps to tell him Congress had just voted in his favor. Congress had not even been in session on that day and the bunch of urchins who planned the practical joke giggle and grimace like gnomes under the Capitol's portico. The last stance of Cendrars's hero is strikingly symbolic: standing erect against the backdrop of the Capitol's steps he raises his arms and falls headlong to his death.

Granted the unabashed use of melodrama, the stylistic leanness and concentration throughout on the cataclysmic destruction of a life dream, add vibrancy and power to the story of the rise and fall of the legendary adventurer. It takes on the apocalyptic tone of a parable of modern greed where God and Mammon are the real protagonists and the hero acquires a timeless mythic stature.

Cendrars, however, was more interested in shaping his own myths than reviving ancient ones. In his treatment of "the marvelous story of General Sutter" (the subtitle of the novel), there is an underlying nostalgia for the old pioneering days. This allegory of greed also reads as an epic of a dying race of adventurers of which

Sutter is one of the last scions. As other Cendrars heroes, Sutter functions successfully only outside of society or as a demiurgic organizer of his own dream world. The very first image of the solitary traveller who incites nothing but hostility and suspicion from the villagers of Runenberg is strikingly symbolic. On his Westward journey he does not wait to join a convoy but is determined to proceed alone heading his own tiny caravan. And on closer inspection his ultimate financial and spiritual ruin is not as much brought about by the ironic fate of the discovery of gold as by an inner congenital inadequacy to cope with historical and social reality:

He could again make a fortune, speculate, take advantage of the skyrocketing rise of food prices; but what the hell. . . . Others will make a fortune. He lets go. He does nothing, (p. 196)

writes Cendrars in one of his rare authorial interjections in this narrative. Like all other cosmic gamblers and tempters of destiny in the Cendrarian mythology, Sutter is an inveterate loner of the breed akin to the seven uncles of *Panama,* Moravagine, Dan Yack, and Galmot, dreamers of world-encompassing fantasies who become fugitives or victims in the anonymity of the modern mass.

Sutter's destiny provides a prototypical pattern for the future novels of Cendrars. Therefore this first brief narrative is of seminal importance in the gradual elaboration of Cendrars's mythology. In spite of consummate narrative craftsmanship and the percussive vigor of the style, *L'Or* is nevertheless not representative of Cendrars's contribution to the art of fiction. It lacks the modernity of form and scope of invention of the subsequent writings. It may seem ironical that fame favored the least original piece of work of Cendrars. The extraordinary instant and lasting popularity of the work (forty-eight editions have appeared so far in fifteen languages) cannot, however, be accounted for only by the fact that it is the most accessible of Cendrars's prose writings. It might be interesting for a sociologist of literature to find out what conscious or unconscious yearnings Cendrars's epic tale satisfied in the readers of this postmodern age. For the critic the fact that Cendrars's effort in this first piece of fiction was not directed toward the search for a new topic, nor a new form, but was a deliberate recasting of a pre-existing document, *L'Or* will remain a necessary stepping stone in the elaboration of Cendrars's relationship to the writing phenomenon.

II   Moravagine: *Destructivity and Destruction of a Hero*

Sutter was an oldtime adventurer of a bygone era. With *Moravagine*, published the following year, Cendrars launched on the literary scene one of the most phenomenal mind and soul shattering hero-monsters ever created, a prototype of the psychotic genius, a force of nature possessed with the revolutionary spirit of a Netchaev, as well as a Jack the Ripper endowed with an unusually acute poetic sensitivity, a character one might expect in days when Dada and Surrealism had made fashionable the case for madness against the rational order.

Before we are introduced to this "superb individual" who, the narrator tells us, "was going to make [him] attend such a show of revolution and transformation, the general upheaval of all social values and life" (vol. 4, p. 70), we are given a formal lecture on the evils of psychiatry and internment in mental institutions which are said to function on behalf of the state police and to organize the systematic destruction of all idealism, all independent thought. The program of the narrator, Raymond la Science, a young intern in a famous Swiss sanatorium, seems directly dictated by the first *Manifesto of Surrealism* in which Breton stated "I could spend my whole life prying loose the secrets of the insane."[4] But Raymond will not be contented with a study *"in vitro"* of his patients in the Pavilion of the Incurables. When he meets Number 1731, a wretched, withered little man with a limp who quietly indulges in masturbation in his room, he is seduced by the voluptuous warmth and color of his voice and recognizes the pride, the contempt, and the sense of grandeur of that solitary and tragic being. He decides to "live in the intimacy of a great human wild beast, observe him, accompany him, share his life" (p. 91) and accordingly plans for his escape from the sanatorium and resigns from his internship.

At first, Moravagine's confessions, only briefly interrupted by Raymond's reports, make up the major portion of the narrative. Moravagine is presented as a victim of history. The last heir to the Hungarian throne, born prematurely on the day of his father's assassination, he had spent all his life—from the incubator to the Waldensee Sanatorium—in complete reclusion. When he was sequestered in the castle of Fejervar, under the guard of Austrian soldiers, he learned how to turn his vital energies inward and developed into an ecstatic hypersensitive dreamer whose self was absorbed into things around him. Married at six to a little princess of the same age, he fell passionately in love with her eyes and henceforth, between fits of rage and despondency, lived only for her yearly visits on their wedding anniversary. The intensity of his passion led him to frantic acts of violence which ranged from periodic stabbings of his own leg, cutting out all the eyes from portraits in the castle gallery, gouging his dog's eyes and crushing the animal to death with a chair, to an unsuccessful attempt to escape that left him a cripple for life and culminated in the disembowelling of his wife, Rita when she told him that she had come to visit him for the last time. He was then eighteen years old. The next ten years of his life were spent in a cell of the fortress of Pressburg from which he was secretly transferred to the Waldensee mental asylum and classified as an incurable case.

In the dark, airless solitude of his cell in the Pressburg prison the young prisoner had learned to seek comfort in a systematic heightening of his sensory perceptions until he reached a peak of synesthetic sensitivity that allowed him "to capture the most beautiful form of silence." (p. 100) As if to prove that the line between artistic and psychotic awareness is only tenuous, Cendrars endowed his hero with the visionary power of a *"Poète maudit."* Moravagine's evocation of his visions in the chapter "The shaping of my mind" belongs to the tradition of Lautréamont, the Rimbaud of *Season in Hell,* or Artaud. The pathological condition, however, took over, assailed Moravagine with hallucinations and all possible varieties of psycho-sensorial disturbances which made him regress to the state of an amoebic existence and suffer crises of personality transgression to the point of identifying himself with a nail in the wall of his cell.

Once freed by Raymond, Moravagine does not wait to justify his pseudonym (Mor-a-vagin(e)—equals death of the vaginus) and immediately stabs a little girl who was gathering dead wood at the foot of the sanatorium's wall. During the succeeding ten years of globe-trotting he will strew women's corpses wherever he goes, and "often in jest," as Raymond comments. After three years devoted to studies in Berlin, Moravagine discovers that the acquisition of knowledge does not help him to find an objective justification for his being. He relapses into a demential condition and becomes the terror of Berlin and its suburbs where young girls and children are disembowelled every night.

Fleeing from Berlin, the pair arrives in Moscow at the end of the Russian-Japanese war whereupon the private history of Moravagine turns into a detailed account of the 1905 Revolution of which he becomes the active life principle, the central brain power of its Europe-wide network of terrorist activity. When his plot to assassinate the czar fails, Raymond and Moravagine start on a fantasmagoric quest journey through various countries. The novel then becomes a series of vignettes in which Moravagine appears to be a mere pretext for Cendrars's irresistible attraction to travel stories.

It is characteristic that the underlying theme of this imaginative travelogue are the oppositions and contrasts between the old World with its *"formules étriquées"* and the New World throbbing with the mechanized rhythm of new industry, on one hand; and between the superrational order and organization of the Western culture and the magic of Amazonia, "the cradle of humanity" on the other. England with its courteous civility is merely a resting place for the exhausted revolutionaries. America, in spite of a lyrical eulogy of its "principle of utility" has no use for the talents of a Moravagine. The episode with the Southwest Indians, a stereotypical far-West adventure of search for a treasure of gold, is a mere springboard for the epic escape up the Orenoque into the heart of Amazonia. In this land of forbidding jungles and swamps, the travellers are captured by the Jivaro Indians. Moravagine, drawn into the organic rhythms of primitive life is raised to the status of god-man. He stages a mass ritualistic sacrifice and with the aid of all the women of the tribe whom he has enslaved with his uncanny powers and sexual magnetism, then arranges to escape with Raymond on board a Portuguese freighter.

Back in France, where the bureaucratic bourgeoisie is scathingly stigmatized, Raymond symptomatically returns to his studies and meditation while Moravagine finds a "new life" in the pioneering world of aviation. When the Second World War breaks out, Moravagine seizes the opportunity as a war pilot to take revenge against Francois Joseph and, contrary to military orders, bombards Vienna's Hofburg. He is forced down by the Austrians. The cycle of the saga is completed when Raymond finds Moravagine, toward the end of the war, in the cell of a military mental hospital. He is now an inveterate morphine addict who imagines himself on Mars and is feverishly writing *L'An 2013*, "a premonitory anticipation of the atomic era or today's Apocalypse." (postface, p. 293)

To the contemporary reader brought up in a world where the atomic bomb (conceived by Moravagine) is no longer an anticipation, where international terrorism and concentration camps are featured in daily headlines, and where a teratological imagination has been almost exhausted by the display of physical and mental distortions of novelists like Vonnegut, Barth or Roth, Cendrars's semipremonitory visions of the collapse of the Western world may appear less than startling. Several critics concurred with Jacques Henry Levesque to see in it a potpourri of the Dada spirit. Indeed no Dada theme is missing: violence, erotic perversion, victory of the irrational, gratuitous crime, action for action's sake, orgy of revolutionary destruction, praise of modern mechanism, and equal passion for primitive mode of thoughts. The overabundance of these themes reaches such a caricaturish density that Philippe Soupault suggested that the book might constitute Cendrars's revenge against Dada. (vol. 4, p. XI)

This extravagant novel remains a puzzle to its readers. Just as Moravagine, when studying music, wanted to discover the *"noyau autogénérateur de l'oeuvre"* one feels impelled to question the inner creative principle of this piece of fiction. The theory, adopted by J. Chadourne among others, of Moravagine as an alter ego, a *Doppelgänger* whom Cendrars had to exorcise, is a tempting one. It is furthermore substantiated by Cendrars himself who tells us in great detail in his *pro domo* how, first planning *Moravagine* as a mere adventure story, a sequence to *Fantomas,* he literally became possessed by the character:

I wanted to start writing, he had taken my place. He was there, settled deep within me as in an armchair. . . . I nourished a parasite at my expense. . . . He travelled in my stead. He made love instead of me. . . . That's why all beautiful books are alike. They are all autobiographical. (p. 280)

Cendrars even carries his facetious confession as far as quoting the letter of a doctor friend of his who praises him for having liberated himself from his double. (p. 291)

The autobiographical elements are of course as numerous as they are transparent. Cendrars had been a medical student like Raymond and had studied music as Moravagine did. The dates of Moravagine's stay in Russia are the same as those of Cendrars's first visit there. Moravagine's arrival in Paris in 1912 and his disappointment with that "nation which the whole world envies" coincides strangely, both in time and spirit, with Cendrars's own return from New York. Although the chapter on Mascha (a Russian revolutionary whom Moravagine impregnates) is strongly tinted with Rémy de Gourmont's *Physique de l'Amour* and Bloch's *La vie sexuelle de notre temps*, [5] there is no need for psychoanalysis to perceive a relationship between the long digression on the masochism of love and Cendrars's own personal crisis after abandoning his first Polish wife with two children. On another level of correspondences, Mascha is the author of a book on the "Perpetual Movement" and Cendrars himself had written on the same topic a few years before. There is also an obvious parallel between Raymond's mutilation during the war and his own; and, although Cendrars never went to the Amazon, he was just coming back from Brazil and had obviously read all possible literature on the subject.

The very fact, too, that the book contains many digressive purple patches would tend to prove that, once the author was freed from his obsessive double, his inspiration flagged and he needed the external geographical, medical, ethnological material that fills the last chapters. Cendrars again backs this impression with his own comments on the genesis of the volume which he condemns for its *"morceaux de bravoure"* and its *"style ampoulé et prétentieux"* (pp. 284, 286), telling us of the trouble he had to patch up pieces when, after several years of interruption, he could not "get back into the spirit of Moravagine." (p. 286)

The novel does read at times like an artificially assembled literary patchwork. True anthology pieces of the best Cendrarian poetic lyricism such as the description of Moscow on the eve of the revolution or the forbidding evocation of the Amazonian swamps are juxtaposed with obvious parodies or barely disguised plagiarism. Rimbaldian tones are easily recognized in the passage on the tactile quality of vowels and consonants (p. 101). Moravagine's declaration of his destructive mission ("I am not of your race. . ." pp. 101–102) seems directly inspired by Alexander Blok's poem *The Scythians* (1918). The stereotypical account of the revolutionary violence is reminiscent of similar episodes in Andreev and Pilnyak. Recent research has, in fact, disclosed several sources of inspiration for both the character of Moravagine and several themes discussed in the novel. As Jay Bochner pointed out, Cendrars's knowledge of the German psychoanalyst Otto Gross largely accounts for the psychic distortions of Moravagine whose revolutionary activities may owe something to accounts of the life of Azev (a member of both the police and the Terrorist brigade) which Cendrars must have read. [7] The parallels between the chapter K entitled "Mascha" and Ivan Bloch's *The Sexual Life of our Time* are as striking as Cendrars's previous borrowings from LeRouge and Birman. Other such disclosures will probably continue to shift the emphasis from Cendrars's creative imagination to his art of imparting a poetic afflatus to pre-existing material. The very care with which Cendrars forestalls the critic by playing the game of candidly disclosing the genesis of his work, should warn of his deliberate conceit.

The object of the exorcism in the creation of *Moravagine*, however, appears to be less an autobiographical phantasm embodied in the hero than the devouring creative urge to codify the myths of contemporary reality. The scope of the author's ambition is made clear by the alphabetical listing of the chapters. The intent is to exhaust the spectrum of forces at work in the modern world from A to Z. This tends to obscure the main charge of the novel which is not the portrait of a man but the author's confrontation with an idea. The idea is that the disappearance of a stable, rational reality which becomes the central experience in our century has now brought about a new society of men addicted to the spirit of violence and collective hysteria spreading throughout the postNietzschean world. For Cendrars, as he stated in his "Note on the Novel," what chiefly characterized modernity was "the deep transformation of today's man" which "cannot be accomplished without a general cataclysm of consciousness and an intimate disruption of the senses and the heart." (vol. 6, p. 35)

This deep transformation is embodied in the novel's hero, a destroyer of mankind for whom modern history provides a suitable field of action. Early on, Cendrars attempts to create, in a *Bildungsroman* fashion, a monstrous human being, amoral, endowed with abnormal propensities, whom he is obviously preparing for extraordinary feats. When the reader first meets Moravagine, isolated in a madman's cell, he is a kind of nonperson in his own society, grounded in passivity, distinguished only by the singular nature of his psychic disturbance. It is not until he comes into contact with the radical dislocation of normal life rhythms in the underground swell of the revolution in Russia, the frenzied rituals of a primitive cult and finally the inflationary spiral of World War I destruction, that Moravagine achieves his stature of a demoniac hero. The brutal primitivism, cruelty, and anarchy generated within these worlds respond to the irrational urges in Moravagine's nature and concretize them into immediate action. He is recreated by the events. In this sense Cendrars reverses the Galahad-slaying-the-dragon image through the hero's fusion with the dragon's evil for his own survival and final transcendence into an integral and dominating destructive force.

"He was the master of us all" says Raymond, "Parturition of a human being, too human, super human, tropism or extreme deprivation . . ./he could/ act without scruples, without remorse, without hesitation or trouble and shed blood in total confidence, as a creator, indifferent like God, indifferent like an idiot." (p. 140)

It is that sub- or superhuman quality of "indifference" that identifies Moravagine with the prevailing chaos of contemporary life. His mocking laughter resounds throughout the work; it underscores the futility of restraining various forms of violence which are purposeless and yet packed with energies, embracing nothingness in a gathering momentum of destruction and self-destruction. He vehemently objurgates Raymond's scholarly pursuits:

Good God, you still need to reflect upon things. . . . You have not yet understood that the world of thought is done for. . . . All is nothing but disorder, my dear fellow. Vegetals, minerals and animals, all is disorder as well. Disorder in the multitude of human races. . . . There is nothing but action . . . antagonistic action. (p. 242)

Moravagine plunges exultantly into the hallucinating "disorder" of existence which reaffirms modern man's inherent violence and his bond with the organic lawlessness of all creatures of the earth. Caught and held in the widening movement of global forces so inhuman and limitless as to turn into an abstraction, the hero becomes an almost purely mythical character. Abruptly the highly charged fantasy is turned off when Cendrars decides to demote his hero from his high position in the "new society of men" for his single, purely human gesture of private vengeance. With great imaginative neatness, Moravagine is returned to the ordinary world only to relapse into insanity.

What is of the greatest interest and constitutes the originality and power of the novel is the writer's reciprocal use of public and private phenomena to develop his major theme. Considered separately, the hero and the happenings do not reach beyond the confines of a sensational adventure story. By fusing the two elements into the interlocking dynamics of action, at once draining and fulfilling,

Cendrars succeeds in projecting, within a conventional episodic structure, a shattering vision of human and inhuman forces about to reshape our world. In such a demiurgic attempt, the intertextual play—which even includes quotations from Cendrars's own previous works—and the lack of an apparent "self generating core" in the novel, appear to take on a very specific significance. The myth is not only the "adventure" narrated or the nature of its hero but the very process of its creation. Hence the necessity for the author ironically to both support and destroy his own mythopoetic construct, inviting the reader to think that writing a book like *Moravagine* "consiste à savoir se procurer de l'argent avec du vent*," but finally providing the most authentic clue to his mythology of a new race:

There is but one topic in literature: man. There is but one literature: that of man, this Other, the man who writes. (p. 280)

III   Dan Yack: *Toward the Frozen Word*

In the wake of Jean Louis Parrot, one of the first critics to attempt a full account of *Dan Yack,* for many years commentators of Cendrars have viewed *Moravagine* and *Dan Yack* as "the two poles between which Cendrars's thought and his novels oscillate," the destructive force of the former hero being seen in contrast to the constructive features of the latter.[8] More recent studies have discarded this point of view as oversimplistic. But, whereas *Moravagine* is being made the key work from which can be deciphered the entire structure of the Cendrarian "*écriture,*"[9] *Dan Yack* increasingly eludes analyses. A recent article of Claude Leroy, however, emphasizes the centrality of the novel in the overall structure of Cendrars's production and suggests that the relative eclipse it has undergone (to the point of a quasi disappearance from the publisher's market) may ironically be due to this very pivotal position.[10]

Published in two volumes in 1929, *Le Plan de l'Aiguille* and *Les Confessions de Dan Yack,* the work was then received as a novel of escape and adventure. "Escape is becoming a standard topic of literature. Before the fashion disappears, let us hurry and admire the works it inspires," wrote Raoul Celly in a review of *Le Plan.*[11]

In the first part, the saga of a voyage to the Antarctic seemed to follow the older tradition of sea voyages (Poe's *Adventures of*

Gordon Pym, Stevenson, Conrad). It also echoed the more recent attraction of the Arctic stimulated by Scott's expedition, popular travel books such as Louis Boussenard's *Les Francais au pôle nord* (1927), press accounts of Russian industrial settlements in the North Pole. Jay Bochner mentions Sir Douglass Mawson's *Home of the Blizzard* (1915) as a possible source. It is probable that Cendrars was also familiar with the recent Russian novels of Zamyatin, *To the North* (1922) and Leonid Leonov's *Egorushka's Undoing* (1923). The topic was in fashion and it was to be expected that in line with the legend of Cendrars's travels attention was then primarily drawn to the apparent superstructure of the narrative as an "adventure story-book."

Events, indeed, are not lacking either in number or extravagance in the Antarctic saga of the first volume or in the recollections of the *Confessions de Dan Yack. Le Plan de l'Aiguille,* which Jay Bochner describes as "the end of a Bildungsroman"[12] is structurally the diachronic third person narrative of a section in the life of its eccentric hero, Dan Yack. The novel opens flamboyantly with the hero's spectacular drunken slide on his shoulder blades across the polished floor of an exclusive Saint Petersburg club. Heir to a multimillionaire's British whaling fleet, Dan Yack is the most famous reveler in town, envied by all of Saint Petersburg, a prototype of the "dandy" living at the turn of the century. The atmosphere captured in the first chapter is also that of the carefree "*fin de siècle.*"

Wobbling through the city, Dan Yack is passed by a carriage from which his former mistress Hedwiga throws him a note informing him of her forthcoming marriage to a Russian prince. Abandoned by his lover and in a state of drunken stupor, Dan Yack lands in a cabaret where, sprawled out under a table, he overhears the conversation of three impoverished artists. In a superbly Romantic gesture, the forsaken lover, who, characteristically, has decided to shake off his past and leave for the farthest reaches of the world, invites the three artists to join him on a voyage to the South Pole on board his schooner, the *Green Star,* and to live for a year on a deserted Antarctic island. The sea voyage is briefly and soberly sketched and the story swiftly moves on to the life of these four men and a dog, alone on one of the Balleny Islands, Sturge Island (called Struge in the novel). They have settled for the sixty-five-day stretch of the long polar winter night in a low cabin composed of two storing areas, one for coal, one for food, and a common room divided into four cubby-holes in which each of them could be "at home so to speak, meditate, think, live, read, write or sleep and digest, isolated behind a tarred sailcloth hung on a rod." (vol. 5, pp. 89–90)

A month hardly goes by before the experiment proves to be a failure. Dan Yack's partners cannot maintain their identity away from their usual environment and they each undergo a gruesome process of physical and mental disintegration until with the return of the sun a raging hurricane brings their ordeal to a spectacular end. Lamont, the composer, who had been "rotting away" with syphilis is drowned with the dog Bari as he attempts to escape on the melting ice floes. Goischman, the poet, dying of scurvy, ends in a fit of madness, when he cuts his nose off and offers it to Dan Yack who, as he runs away, horrified, leaving the door open, causes the blizzard to overturn the stove and thus sets the whole settlement ablaze with Goischman burnt alive in it. Sabbakof, the sculptor, had been kept "sane" by his dream of the perfect statue he could carve in pure ice when the sun returns. But he falls victim to his passion and, during that same fatal hurricane, is crushed by the statue he had carved of Dan Yack.

Dan Yack alone survives on the island in a state of dazed or indifferent self-fulfillment where aside from himself, a snow petrel and a sea elephant are the only signs of life. When the Green Star comes to pick him up the frenzy of life takes over again. In the island of Chiloe (off the coast of Chile), Dan Yack treats himself and his crew to an orgy of sex, gambling, food and wine, exultation over blaring music machines. He then plunges headlong into the establishment of a multidimensional whaling industry consortium, creates a model industrial town called "community city" in which he "wanted to establish a kind of universal happiness." (p. 183) The text reads like a modern fairy tale of a new world success story. But Dan Yack's euphoria does not last through the seventh winter. In the midst of his booming success he drifts into a state of indifference to it, is haunted by the idea of death and the need for love. His life suddenly appears to him as the capsizing iceberg he is watching from his seal hunting boat:

He too, from now on, would go, keel upwards and slowly melt, gradually crumble away and suddenly vanish into fetid glairy brine. . . . Be scattered, broken up, and like that porous iceberg, suddenly dissolve into nothingness. (p. 192)

The second volume, *Les Confessions de Dan Yack*, contains the recollections of the hero's past. It is a meditative pause after the explosion of action in the first volume, the "expression of experience" following "the absorption of experience" as Jay Bochner puts it, commenting upon the often quoted statement of Cendrars on the binary character of his novel:

The World is my representation. I wanted to interiorize in Dan Yack this mental outlook, which is a pessimistic point of view, then exteriorize it, which is an optimistic action.

Hence the division in two parts of my novel; the first one, from outside to inside, subject of *Le Plan de L'Aiguille*; from inside to outside, object of *Les Confessions de Dan Yack*, the second one. Systole, diastole: the poles of existence. Outside in, inside out [in English in the original], the two beats of the mechanical movement. . . ."[13]

The dualism of the narrative is carried even further in the internal structure of the *Confessions*. Allegedly recorded on a dictaphone, the book is presented as a succession of reels in which the memories of Dan Yack alternate with the diaries of his deceased wife, Mireille, thus affording the reader a double angle of vision on his past.

Roughly a decade after the whaling industry episode in Port Deception, Dan Yack is back in the solitude of icebound lands, this time in a chalet at *Le Plan de l'Aiguille*, a glacier near Chamonix which, ironically enough, Cendrars had chosen as the title for the Antarctic saga. Once more, he is left alone after a death for which he is indirectly responsible. The first reel opens with his difficulty to voice the fact of Mireille's death and his desire to recall his entire past. The memory of his gentle and platonic love for this innocent ethereal being—perhaps the most poignant description of brotherly-fatherly feelings to be found in all literature—is mingled in a semi-erratic fashion with evocations of the war he had experienced, erotic experiments of his past, his neurotic passion for killing seals, meditations on alienation, encounters with local inhabitants at the village bar, etc. Mireille's diaries start with a moving childlike narrative of her life with her dying father. They inform both Dan Yack and the reader of the uncanny spiritual devastation hidden behind the "simple" ethereal love. The purity of the relationship is in the innocent laughter that Dan Yack, whom she calls *"mon grand,"* knew how to bring out in her. It is recalled throughout the reels as a leitmotiv. Dan Yack learns, however, that the mysterious psychosomatic illness, of which he had hoped to cure her when he launched her as an actress in the motion picture company he had created in her own name *(Société Mireille)*, had actually been aggravated when he had her cast in the part of Gribouille. The role of this wretched little fellow was too closely locked in with her own identity. It destroyed her through a shock of recognition of her true self:

It was so much me that I felt as though I was acting naked, totally naked, morally naked. (p. 267)

Suddenly the chaste purity of her love for Dan Yack, of which she was proud, appears to her as the result of her sexual ambiguity and she sees his love as nothing but pity. The source of all her happiness has become the object of her fear.

After reading Mireille's last diary, Dan Yack returns to his memories of Hedwiga, of whose death he has learned through a chance encounter with a former revelling companion, and he turns back once more to his thoughts of the war and the "sexual erotic disorientation" it entailed.

The *Confessions* end with a new beginning for the hero who emerges from all his experiences as intact as ever, starting a new life in a Paris apartment in which he has knocked down all the partitions except those enclosing the bathroom, where he keeps a tortoise. While indulging in a most elaborate modernistic light system he camps in a hammock and cooks on a wood fire. He has adopted a son who reminds him of Hedwiga and his new mission in life is to teach him how to laugh.

In spite of the superabundant wealth of "material for narrative construction," to apply the Russian Formalists' distinction between "fabula" and "plot,"[14] the driving force of the narrative escapes any diachronic linear reading. The very disparity of various summaries attempted, including this one, illustrates the necessity to search for a level of significance beyond the anecdotic. Most commentators have agreed with J. L. Parrot who pointed out that "the secret plan" of the book can only "be defined if that novel is read as a spiritual odyssey, which it is actually, and not as an adventure story book."[15] Indeed, contrary to more conventional fiction, instead of furthering the plot or developing characters the hero's experience seem rather to furnish the empty spaces of the novel. The reader's feeling at the end of the work is rather that expressed by another poet of far distances, Segalen: "as always one made a journey far away from what was nothing but a journey into the depth of the self."[16]

The temptation of a metaphysical interpretation is strong, and Cendrars himself, in one of his numerous auto-commentaries on his work, suggested such a direction: "There is but one character and everything takes place in his mind." (vol. 6, p. 153) The question then arises whether *Dan Yack* is a personal spiritual odyssey, a voyage into the inner space of the author's self or whether the odyssey of the self embodied in *Dan Yack* is a visionary projection of the spirit of the age.

Dan Yack, the protagonist, has often been hailed as the prototype of the modern man. Cendrars himself, in turn, both promoted and demoted the idea. His dedication to Abel Gance states:

Don't look [in this novel] for a new art formula or a new mode of writing, but truly for the expression of the general state of health of to-morrow. . . . (vol. 5, p. 53)

Thirty years later he expressed a similar idea in speaking of his character as "this most modern, most unhinged hero in the century,"[17] whereas in 1950 he had sneered at Robert Mannoll's query as to whether Dan Yack should be viewed as the symbol of modern man:

No, do you really believe in that business of the symbol of modern man? (vol. 13, p. 25)

In many ways Dan Yack fulfills the part admirably. There is about him the dehumanized unemotionality, the spiritual sterility, the abysmal unconscious void of a self-propelled mechanism maintained in motion by the externality of actions and objects that dominate him but do not establish for him any ontological relationship with the world. There is a striking resemblance between him and the new being whom the French sociologist Henri Lefebvre describes as the "*cybernanthrope.*" Just as the *cybernanthrope* is both fascinated and awed by the technological achievements of cybernetics, Dan Yack is spellbound by the gadgetry of his age. He immediately introduces himself to the three artists he is inviting on his Antarctic voyage as a man who knows nothing about fine arts, never reads a book, is bored by music and only likes "the nasal whine of a phonograph and the terrific din of a gramophone." "One thing you can bet on" he warns them, "is that I will take along a cargo load of cylinders and records, as well as half a dozen of elaborate machines." (p. 73) His favorite recording is that of the howling of a fur seal being slaughtered. On the island of Chiloe he is totally mesmerized by all the gramolas, the automatic picture machines, automatic rifles, and cock shies of the gambling rooms. He is so obsessed by a mechanical orchestra of stuffed cats that he plays it night after night until it breaks and then orders one from Europe for his new home in "Community City." In the second volume a dictaphone is his new toy and when he starts a new life in his empty Paris apartment he surrounds himself with flood box lights, surgeon's lamps, neon tubes, a vapor lamp device which projects his name on the ceiling and "were it not for the neighbors" he "would install a whole system of sirens or . . . samples of all types of electric horns and would have fun making them work all night long." (p. 313)

His sexual immaturity, expressed by his double failure in love— whether sensual with Hedwiga or platonic with Mireille—his obsession with chastity and his compulsive eroticism pertain to a similar externalization of desire in the form of a mechanistic consumerism of objects. Lefebvre describes the *cybernanthrope* as a man who:

ignores desire. If he recognizes it, it is to elude it. He has nothing but needs. That need is distinctly and clearly the need for this or that. He satisfies himself through consuming this or that, doing this or that. . . . For the cybernanthrope, desire becomes localized and specialized eroticism.[18]

References to Dan Yack's erotic needs or past experiences recur throughout the two volumes, but no better illustration of Lefebvre's point can be found than the episode of the *"guesquel"* during his frantic orgy of sex with Indian women on Chiloe island. In this respect it is characteristic that when Dan Yack is bereft of all his belongings after the blizzard on Struge Island he remains fundamentally unperturbed and his greatest experience in that ordeal is precisely the discovery of a state of desirelessness:

He had no worries of any kind. The only thing that bothered him at times was his chastity. . . . He had no fire, no tobacco and yet he did not miss anything. He did not desire anything. He was not expecting anything. (pp. 140–41)

A need requires external stimulus whereas desire springs from the inner core of the being, which is precisely what is lacking in Dan Yack. At no time in the novel does one feel that Dan Yack's actions are propelled by any kind of inner motivation. In the three instances of what is generally viewed as his positive constructive nature he almost mechanically and by chance reacts to a sense of the needs in others, offering them only what is in his power to provide, that is material benefits or external circumstances. Liberating the three artists from the grip of hunger and the search for a roof each night as well as from social pressures around them leads to complete psychic disintegration and finally death. His dream of establishing "a kind of universal happiness" in Community City turns into the creation of a successful industrial laboratory. But it becomes a dehumanized futuristic world which reduces him to a state of depression only lifted by the sadistic overkilling of seals. Similarly, everything that he lavishly spends on Mireille, when he launches a motion picture company to bring out her talent brings on her death instead. He not only fails in changing lives for the better but even destroys them because he cannot fulfill the totality of being that desires to be brought out in each individual, since he himself remains external to the roots of being in his world of actions and artifacts.

What probably best epitomizes the modern desensitization and dissociation from life forces embodied by Dan Yack is his famous laughter which resounds throughout the first volume and remains with him in the second volume as his best gift to Mireille as well as the one thing he has to teach his son. That huge burst of laughter which sweeps everything away is Dan Yack's most characteristic means of expressing and, at the same time, escaping the irrationalism he senses in the world and himself. In a long author's aside on the hero's state of mind at the end of the first volume, Cendrars qualifies such "wanton laughter" as "the new regime of personality," (p. 194) thus unequivocally granting his hero the status of a key agent in the realization of the goals he had set for the novel in the same terms a few years earlier (See p. 76).

The writer himself, critics and a new image of the human psyche as subsequently perceived by sociologists conjoin to make of Dan Yack a symbol of modernity. Dan Yack's exodus to the frozen world of the Antarctic and his own spiritual void can indeed be interpreted as the odyssey that Parrot perceived in it. It might rather be viewed as an anti-odyssey since there is no development or change of the being through experience but, nonetheless, a symptomatic interpretation of the state of contemporary man.

Such an interpretation also fits within the general framework of the mythopoetic intent of the author of "Profond Aujourd'hui" in which Cendrars is viewed as fusing into his creative network inner and outer knowledge of the self and the world, experience, and vision. Just as *Moravagine* can be read as the exorcism of an alter ego, *Dan Yack* may be considered as the fantasized self of Cendrars in his role of the "most contemporary of contemporaries" as Henry Miller saw him. There are enough instances of autobiographical transpositions to uphold the alternative interpretation of *Dan Yack* as a personal spiritual odyssey, suggested earlier. Dan Yack's craze for gramophones, dictaphones, automatons is but a hyperbolic version of Cendrars's own fascination with technological wizardry. So does the establishment of a multinational consortium recall Cendrars's own attempts to launch a big import-export project upon his return from Brazil. The creation by Dan Yack of a motion picture company gave Cendrars an outlet for the expression of his own experience with the film world. Dan Yack's nagging memory of the war is evidently also Cendrars's. Mireille is a barely disguised portrayal of Raymone. The location of the Plan de l'Aiguille in the Alps is the place where Cendrars had worked with Abel Gance for the shooting of *La Roue* and the self-willed exile on an Antarctic island can be seen as a poetic transposition of Cendrars's own frequent spells of hibernation from the world whether it was in an unknown country retreat or in an anonymous hotel room.

A more subtle parallel can be traced on a psychological level if one compares the novel with *Une nuit dans la forêt*, the first piece of acknowledged autobiography that Cendrars published the same year. The description that Cendrars makes of himself as a "Brahmin in reverse who contemplates himself in agitation," a man for whom there is "no philosophical conception of contempt for life more complete and absolute than action. . . ." Action which "always springs out of contingencies, disinterestedly and selfishly" (vol. 6, pp. 138–39), is more than applicable to the character of Dan Yack. A similarly tempting parallel can be drawn between Cendrars's hero and the perceptive portrayal of the author made by his friend Henry Miller:

He goes through metamorphosis without surrendering his identity. . . . He experiences in his soul genuine eclipses. He knows what it means to fly off at a tangent, or to sweep across the sky like a flaming comet. He has been put on the rack, drawn and quartered, he has pursued his own shadow, tasted madness. . . . He is a vital force, a blind and pitiless surge. . . . He is tender and ruthless at the same time. He is antinomian.[19]

Nevertheless, a closer reading of the narrative brings out another level of significance which finally unifies its otherwise heterogeneous features. As a substratum to the "adventure" of the hero one finds a constant concern with the dynamics of the creative process, with the "adventure" of the discourse itself, which meanders through a profusion of stylistic variety to the ultimate experience of silence.

After the exuberant buoyancy of the first chapter in the clubs and cafés of Saint Petersburg, where words pop like champagne corks, the pall of the Arctic silence settles on the very fiber of the text. The avalanche of colorful images of the first pages (an areca compared to a heron on one leg, the raping of the morning's spotless scarf, the bristling surface of the Neva likened to the fur of a cat setting up his back . . .) is succeeded by a verbal staccato of spare and stripped notations. The sea voyage is described with the factual terseness of a logbook:

The setting sun was livid. It was cold. An icy breeze was coming from the Antarctic Pole. The thermometer had dropped two degrees below zero. The next day, same cold, same swell from the South; continuous thick fog; no sun at noon and therefore no bearings.
Storm on the 6th, 7th, 8th, 9th, 10th, 11th and 12th. . . .

(p. 75)

After the fatal blizzard not the slightest emotion is allowed to pierce through the devastation left after the cataclysm:

Charred beams rise from a heap of rubble buried in the snow.
Still snowing.
All is white.
The wind has finally subsided.
What silence (p. 138)

In the description of the hurricane, according to Cendrars, who himself later analyzed his style, sentences "become frozen, cracked, they start to thaw, lose their balance, topple over, explode, drift away, splinter as do the icefloes in the offing." (vol. 13, p. 24)

Beyond the concern with the variety of forms of expression a query of much wider import is gradually delineated. The experiment of life on Struge Island was hardly started when the leading question that haunts the narrative is raised:

What are these words that remained unspoken and who makes an effort to speak? (p. 90)

The identity of both the creative material and the creator is being questioned at the start of the chapter in which the three artists will be destroyed precisely by their inability to determine either or any of these. Lamont's feverish abortive effort to compose, the prostration of the poet Goischman into total silence and the distortion of creative impulse through the idolatory of abstraction in the case of the sculptor Sabbakof reflect facets of the author's creative anguish.

The same inability to find an adequate mode of expression befalls Dan Yack who in addition to all his other characteristics could also be listed in a directory of protagonists of the Novel of Silence. Dan Yack's silence is not only figuratively expressed through his Modernistic behavior analyzed in the preceding pages. It is verbalized throughout the novel. Comments such as:

"The two men had nothing more to tell each other." (p. 119)
"He could not say anything." (p. 120)
"To talk, what a nuisance and what's the point of it? To say what," (p. 147)

punctuate each encounter of Dan Yack with his companions during the Antarctic episode. When he is impelled to express himself to Sabbakof ("He had so many things to tell him"), once stalled by his friend's death, he immediately returns to his inner silence: "What irony! . . . He had nothing more to tell him." (p. 134)

In this light the stylistic and structural volteface of the second volume becomes an inescapable outcome of the inner logic of the narrative. The traditional child's-tale tone of Mireille's diaries stands as a foil to the halty, repetitive discontinuum of Dan Yack's memories. In the first two reels of the *Confessions*, when Dan Yack is pacing up and down his room in a painful effort to "recall everything" and record it in his dictaphone, he bears a striking resemblance to Beckett's character in *Krapp's Last Tape*. Seizing upon any pretext to get up from his table (get tobacco, fill his pipe, fetch a coke, poke the fire, wash his hands, etc.) he remains unable to express the one thing which prompted the confessional return on his past. The unfinished sentence: "I would like to say that . . ." recurs like a leitmotiv, followed by the desperate question: "How to say that Mireille is dead? . . . But how to say it . . . how to say it." (pp. 201–02), until at the end of the second reel he frees himself from the burden by speaking it out to the secretary who will type the reels:

You probably know, Miss, that Mireille is dead? . . .
That is precisely what I wanted to say. . . . Yes. (p. 209)

An interlocutor had to be found to liberate the word, but the actual dialogue will take place with Mireille who is the only one who actually will word her death to him in her diaries.

Dan Yack's withdrawal at the end of the novel into a world of nonverbal communication, running on all fours with a little pink rabbit and his son whom he will teach how to laugh, thus appears as the figuration of a double closure, that of language upon silence and that of the fictional hero who, in the passage from action to contemplation, loses his ontological bearings.

In the final analysis, Cendrars's novel becomes therefore a true odyssey of the narrative which reaches a point of no return. It is not accidental that Dan Yack is the last fictive hero created by Cendrars. Unable to finalize a form of being or a form of expression in the framework of traditional fiction, in this work he had already mapped out his future itinerary: a passage from exteriority to interiority which will lead him from reporting and fantasy to the mythification of his own persona in the fictionalized autobiography of the tetralogy.

IV   Rhum, *the Arraignment of Adventure*

At a time when the creative impetus of the author of *Dan Yack* seemed to have reached a stasis in a frozen land of silence, current events provided Cendrars with a real life paradigm of his hero-adventurers. Commissioned by the Parisian paper *Vu* to write a series of articles on the Guiana *député* Jean Galmot and cover the trial of his murder then taking place in Nantes, Cendrars found a contemporary Sutter. The imaginative writer immediately prevailed over the journalist and by the end of 1930, *Rhum, l'aventure de Jean Galmot* was published by Grasset.

Poisoned in April 1928 in his Guiana home after a native uprising in his favor against a government agent had ensured his election as a mayor, Jean Galmot had at forty-nine years of age ended an extraordinary life of meteoric success and failure. Born in a rather poor family in Périgord, he soon abandoned his family's goal for him to become a teacher for a freelance career with a provincial newspaper in Nice. After lavishly living off his American wife's fortune and squandering it, he was sent by his father-in-law to Guiana.

There, after years of hard struggle in the jungle as a gold prospector, planter, trapper, and rum dealer he became a partner in an import-export trade and gradually grew to achieve the status of a business world tycoon, owner of multinational consortiums in exotic woods, rubber, rum, sugar, and related industries. A defender of the local interests against French government investments he was elected *député* for Guiana at the French *Assemblée Nationale*. At the height of his political and financial success, he was accused in the famous *"Affaire des Rhums"* of making illegal profits on rum imports during the First World War. Imprisoned in Paris for months, he became bankrupt and was even divested of his parliamentary allowance. Once out of prison, teetering on the edge of physical and financial ruin, he still managed to pay his fine to the French government and went back to Guiana to campaign for reelection. Although the people of Guiana loved him and he had "vowed his heart" to that nation, he returned to a nest of political intrigues which led him to his fatal end.

The parallels between the destinies of Jean Galmot and the Swiss martyr of the Gold Rush are striking and were bound to capture Cendrars's mind and heart. We find again the same pattern of a dizzyingly successful ascent that lifts a boldly enterprising adventurer only to see him hurled down into failure and harrassment by the forces of collectivity and government institutions. The theme is treated by Cendrars with the same swift sparseness of style he used in *Sutter's Gold*. Only brief notations such as the following mark the progress of Jean Galmot:

Gold, tulipwood, and aromatic plant oils and balata. And if he has to build: he will build. Oil distilleries, sugar refineries. Sugar and rum. And if he must plant, he will plant. Sugar canes will fill up cargo holds. And rum, rum, tons of rum for white men on the other side of the earth. He will be rich.

. . .

1908, 1909, 1910, 1911, 1912, 1913.

He struggles. He has never yielded and he has started over again and again. And chance finally comes to him. (vol. 6, pp. 210, 211)

The episodes of his life in the equatorial jungle brought back to Cendrars his travel notes style of *Documentaires* in paratactic enumerations of the flora and fauna of the area. But just as he avoided having to expand on Sutter's sea voyages or Westward trek, Cendrars reduced to the utmost the exotic flavor which the topic so richly offered. The danger and threat of the forest, the undermining force of malaria, the subhuman conditions of work in muddy marshes are powerfully but briefly evoked. What dominates Cendrars's narrative is the solitude of his protagonist who is projected as a frail quixotic figure standing alone—in the jungle, among men at work, as a magnate of industry, in his prison cell, in his court trials—and finally in death.

Numerous pieces of realistic reportage such as Galmot's letters and those of his friends, press excerpts, quotations from the speeches of the lawyers for the defense, seem to authenticate the objectivity of the text, but *Rhum* is not a creatively written journalistic account, nor is it only the fictional chronicling of a public event. The writer reaches into another dimension when the novel becomes an impassioned requisitory against the forces at work to destroy the philanthropist colonial builder whom Cendrars sees in Galmot. The author's bias seems to override the facts. The general effect is that of a black and white picture in which the worlds of finance, justice, the press, the police, the government officials are seem as murky, lawless embodiments of evil against the romantically idealized pure champion of individual rights who to his downfall "believed in the justice of his country" (p. 246) and "put his trust in legality" (p. 281).

Was such muckraking of government agencies and anti-individual forces of the modern world the reason why Cendrars dedicated this volume to "the young men of to-day, tired of literature, to prove to them that a novel can also be an act" (p. 178)? In addition to the similarities with the case of Sutter, Galmot could also have attracted Cendrars for personal reasons. A quick glance at his biography reveals that Cendrars had frequently been torn between his loner's vocation as a writer and a need for active participation in spectacular enterprises (publishing, movie world, active service in the two world wars, founding an import-export company, etc.). His dream of making a fortune in import-export trade with Brazil in 1928, although shortlived, might have been sufficient motivation to arouse Cendrars's empathy to Galmot's ordeal. Furthermore Galmot was also the author of some novels. However minor—and even unknown—a writer he was, Cendrars repeatedly insists on his admiration for this man of action who from four to seven A.M. always found time to devote himself to his literary pursuits. Such personal investment in the destiny of Galmot could have determined the urge to use writing as a politically and socially vindictive tool, in other words, to turn writing into an "act" of public use.

If this were the case, *Rhum* should be classified as a piece of nonfiction writing in line with the current trends of New Journalism in this country. Yet, as will be seen in the following chapters, even in his more specifically journalistic texts, Cendrars remained first and foremost a fanciful storyteller. His primary concern is of a literary nature and a closer reading projects in *Rhum* a continuation of the questioning as to the very possibility of writing already delineated in Dan Yack.

For a mythmaker such as Cendrars the encounter with the real-life embodiment of the prototypical adventurer of his imagination was to raise the crucial issue of the relationship between fiction and reality, of the function of writing when the process of mimesis is reversed and life imitates art.

In the very first pages of the novel the author interferes with the semi-anguished semi-ironical question:

> A man's life!
> Where does one start? (p. 182)

Only a few lines later the theme of the irreality of the "real life" of his character is immediately brought out:

> "Jean Galmot, what a legend" (p. 182)
> "It was not a myth. That man existed." (p. 184)

As if to authenticate Galmot's reality Cendrars evokes a meeting with him and briefly undertakes to demythify the legendary aspect of the man by sketching the description of an unassuming "tall," "thin," "sickly" man with a "certain peasant-like timidity" and a "pure childlike expression in his eyes." "How far we are from his legend . . . from the laborious inventions of his adversaries" states the writer who then proceeds to inscribe his character in the historical and literary tradition of the conquistadors and Don Quixote and places himself as an author under the aegis of Balzac:

Why don't we do with real characters of life what Balzac used to do with imaginary characters? (p. 185)

Here is a paradoxical way to secure the reality of his character, but also a most revealing illustration of the interplay of literary and actual experience in Cendrars's writing. For someone who believed that "literature is a poetic lie which restores the truth in the eye of the reader" (see first chapter) the hallmark of truth in life needs to be stamped in the intertextuality of literary figures.

The following chapter treats the wider issue concerning the very nature of narration in the depiction of a hero's life. With a certain kind of self-consciousness, as if to constantly remind the reader of the actuality of the events related, Cendrars stresses the novelistic quality of this reporting assignment with an insert such as: "The novel starts. But it is not a novel. It is life. Life." (p. 194) Then, later, he again interrupts his narration, as if to bring the reader back into reality, and remind him once more that he is not reading a piece of fiction:

All this is simple, ordinary, logical and would not be sufficient to fill up the pages of a book. (p. 199)

Such inserts scattered throughout the narrative like a writer's preliminary notes to himself create a subtext in which the act of writing as a subject eclipses its object. The self-refraction process of the creative act is further strengthened by the "play within the play" function of the hero's writings. It is not without ironic purpose that Cendrars singles out the episode of the "*Bandit de Pégomas*" as one of the journalistic feats of Galmot. Through a series of purely invented stories of bandits in the lower Alps near Grasse which Galmot published in the daily paper *Le petit Niçois*, he managed to stir the entire police force and bring about actual banditry in the area, thus proving that mythic creations can become true. Conversely, Galmot, the man of action, the adventurer of the equatorial jungle resorts to writing to actualize an experience which remains irreal until it becomes the object of literary creation:

His life seems irreal to him and . . . to give a greater weight to his personality, to assert himself, he feels the need to "story" himself. . . . He is not sitting by a fire. Fire is blazing in his heart. This is how he writes. *What a strange story* (italics in the original). (p. 209)

While the real life adventurer, Galmot "de-irrealizes" his experience through writing, the writer Cendrars keeps asserting the priority of life over romanticized literary adventure:

He was the man of adventure: and adventure is not what one imagines, a novel. . . . Adventure is always lived and, to know it, one must above all be up to it, to live it, live and not be afraid. (p. 206)

Thus, just as the world was proceeding to the arraignment and the destruction of the adventurer of mythical stature which Galmot represented, Cendrars was actualizing in literature the eclipse of his favorite subject matter.

Relating a conversation he had with a London financeer about Galmot, Cendrars ends his narrative with his interlocutor's remark: "At home, in England, Jean Galmot would have been the Cecil Rhodes of Guiana." Such grandiose figures, however—a Cecil Rhodes or a Sutter—living out a fully exteriorized destiny as loners, belonged to an era which is like a stranger to our own. Cendrars had no illusion either as to the anachronism of freewheeling adventurers in the contemporary world either in reality or within the imaginative setting of a modern novel. Four years later he will sign a contract with Grasset for a book on Jim Fisk to be entitled *L'Argent*, another Sutter-Galmot-like success and failure story. But, characteristically, he will abandon the project. Rather than opening up the series of fictionalized reportings of Cendrars's subsequent writings, *Rhum* marks the closure of his novelistic cycle.

CHAPTER 6

The Novelist Turned Reporter

T HE next decade in Cendrars's life has been viewed mostly as a period of dispersion and creative lull during which, lacking inspiration the author turned to editing, translations, and reporting.[1] Indeed between 1930 and 1935, with the exception of *Vol à Voile*, the short piece of autobiography discussed in the introductory chapter, only three very brief stories appeared in literary magazines.[2] When in 1935 *Paris Soir* sent him with a team of other reporters to cover the inaugural voyage of SS Normandie and the morning daily paper *Le Jour* published his articles on the French underworld, many of his former admirers may have felt that the poet of the modern world had exhausted his creative vein and was reduced to hack writing. On the other hand, in view of the current trends which view journalism as a new art form, one may surmise that Cendrars was once more ahead of his time and like many recent leading novelists was turning to journalism, anticipating Truman Capote's opinion that:

Journalism is really the most avant-garde form of writing existent to-day . . . actually the last great unexplored literary frontier.[3]

Cendrars's more purely reportorial works have been published in three volumes, a collection in a slightly revised form of his articles on the French underworld written for the Paris daily paper *Le Jour* in *Panorama de la pègre* (1935), those on Hollywood commissioned by *Paris Soir* in *Hollywood, la Mecque du cinéma* (1936) and his World War II reportings in *Chez l'armée anglaise* (1940). All three series theoretically belong to the category of documentary journalism. The assumed projected personality of Cendrars would indeed seem particularly suited to the genre. A man who incessantly claimed that writing was not living would be expected to find in reporting assignments the opportunity to combine his love of action, travel, and adventure with his inveterate urge to write. He possessed the sensitive trained observer's eye and hearing ear considered a *sine qua non* for journalism and would readily bring to the profession the creative skills sought for by advocates of New Journalism.[4] But would not the writer who took his motto from the Schopenhaurian formula, "The World is my representation" let his natural mythopoetic inclination opt for a reconstruction of reality as perceived through his mind's eye?

I *Nostalgia For the Journalism of the Gaslight Era:* [Panorama de la Pègre]

The first series, *Panorama de la pègre,* seemed to be a natural for the lover of all kinds of outlaws who had just translated Al Jennings's book *Through the Shadows with O'Henry.* The book describes the various haunts and tactics of the French underworld. Starting in Paris with the "ganglands" of the elegant clubs on the Champs Elysées, the drug traffic and white slave trade of shady bars of the Rue de Douai, Cendrars pursues his investigation in Marseilles, the "world market of opium" with its gambling dens and brothels to which he devotes several chapters. Less famous independent smuggling operations on the Belgian border are also given space as well as picturesque anecdotes about all kinds of weapons, goods, animals, and men being smuggled twenty-four hours a day along the Spanish frontier, often within sight and hearing of police patrols. To complete this survey of underworld activities in France he returns to the Paris gambling dens, the street con men and hired killers.

The coverage of the topic is fairly comprehensive and shows a certain familiarity with this undercover commerce. The treatment of it, however, is not objectively informative. The tone of the investigation is set in the first chapter by the insertion for the fourth time in Cendrars's publications of a passage from one of his favorite pieces on modernity: *"Le principe de l'utilité."*[5] Beyond the habitual trickery of Cendrars's frequent auto-quotations, the recurrence of this text which emphasizes the anonymous character of modern society underscores the author's obsession with the mechanization and collectivization of the modern world. The prevailing climate of the work is Cendrars's personally disappointing discovery that the world beyond the pale of law and order which the adventure story writer imagines to be individually perilous, exciting, and eccentric, is in fact a soberly suited, highly organized collective enterprise run very much on the lines of uniformity and efficiency of a large legally established company. The world Cendrars was yearning to write about was the romantic one of the gaslight era ruffians, of slouch-hatted thieves and prowlers who peopled the nineteenth-century stories of Eugene Sue in *Mystères de Paris*. Obviously more fed by his literary reminiscences than by firsthand observations, Cendrars repeatedly deplores the businesslike anonymity of the modern Mafias which prevents him from indulging in any kind of "literary romanticism." Within the space of two pages alone we find such comments as "Nowadays, this romanticism is totally obsolete," "Such modern promiscuity is radically opposed to any kind of romanticism." (vol. 7, p. 7), and the more explicitly nostalgic note of resignation:

One must admit that the poetry of the underworld is dead and here literary romanticism is out of date. (p. 8)

The poet of modernity who in 1917 had plunged headlong into the "profound to-day" would have actually felt more attuned to the dramatic personal tone of pioneers of literary journalism such as Dickens.

II *Blaise Cendrars in Hollywood*

If the encounter with the modern underworld could have been easily tarnished by literary reminiscences of romantic evocations of that once colorful section of society, a reporting assignment on the world center of motion picture industry would be expected to have been an exhilarating experience for a Cendrars who had ex-perimented in film arts in their pioneering days. Yet the reader who looks for an expert's account of the inner workings of the studios or merely some behind-the-screen revelations about the stars will be faced with the most extravagant piece of imaginary reporting. Not that Cendrars's visit to Hollywood can be "added" to his long list of putative explorations to China, the Antarctic, Africa or the Amazon jungle. Documents prove that he did carry on his investigation in loci and sailed back from San Pedro to Le Havre on board the Wisconsin between February 17 and March 19, 1936.

On the face of it, however, Cendrars the journalist performed an incredible sleight-of-hand reporting stint. He did not penetrate beyond the reception room of United Artists, Paramount or

Goldwyn Meyer, and he did not interview any of the leading directors or artists. Cendrars's Hollywood is presented as a "forbidden city" surrounded by a "Chinese wall" which can only be entered through a few "turnstiles" guarded by gatekeepers whom he compares to Cerberi, the watchdogs of Hades. These custodians and awesome entrances to the studios are described at length. On the other hand, we are told how in passing Cendrars missed an interview with Charles Boyer because he was kept waiting too long by one of these "hypocritical monsters who controlled access to the Paramount," how Charlie Chaplin could not see him because the actor was too nervous and how he did not realize his old wish to meet Louise Fazenda, "the only comic woman on the screen," because she had just given birth to a child. At the United Artists' studios he only ventured an "indiscreet glance" into Mary Pickford's suite and when passed by Douglas Fairbanks in the yard he did not dare stop him. Published pictures show Cendrars with Bette Davis, for instance, but she is not mentioned in his report.

In his introduction to the volume, Raymond Dumay wonders whether these tantalizingly unexpected and partial glimpses into the world of the cinema are meant to be humorous, provocative or simply offered mindlessly to the reader. There is certainly a good deal of humor and provocation in most of Cendrars's writings and in this whimsical reportage they have been allotted their share. On the other hand there is inner logic in all Cendrars's work and he was obeying his deeply rooted conviction that truth is always imaginary. As if to ward off potential criticism Cendrars even inserted his personal *"ars poetica"* of journalism into the volume. In a section entitled *"Importance primordiale de l'actualité"* he makes his position very clear:

I never take notes on a journey . . .
A reporter is not simply a picture hunter, he must know
how to see through the mind's eye . . .
The point is not to be objective. One must take sides.
If he does not put himself into it a journalist will never
succeed in rendering this present day life, which is also
viewed through the mind's eye. (vol. 7, pp. 132, 133)

Thus Cendrars's reporting on Hollywood turns out to be more the reporting of his own journey to California. There are chapters on burglary in New York, on the economic crisis in America (a topic brought about by a chance meeting with the economist Harold Loeb

on the train from Chicago to Los Angeles), descriptions of the
scenery seen through the train window in New Mexico, anecdotes
about his being stopped by the police for walking in the streets of
Hollywood, accounts of his visits to the Los Angeles City Court and
City Hall, etc.

These digressions apart, the spirit of the motion picture universe
is strikingly captured. What caught the mind's eye of the writer was
the "manufacture of illusions" aspect of Hollywood. The labyrinth of
technical departments through which the idea of a scenario is
metamorphosed before it creates the illusion of life on the screen for
thousands of spectators appeared to Cendrars a laboratory of magic.
That industry of make-believe takes on for him a "cosmic," "mystical" dimension. But he is not duped by his own unbridled lyricism.
It is only in half mockery that Cendrars describes his feelings of
exultation when he sees on the stage set of The Big Ziegfeld Follies
the "formal and live representation" (vol. 7, p. 173) of a monument
described in his novel *Dan Yack*. The only difference is that "this
monument of plastic synthesis and apotheosis of life" (p. 172) dreamt
of by his hero, the sculptor Sabbakoff, was crowned by Prometheus
whereas, in Hollywood, Prometheus has become an "adorable
brunette." In Hollywood, one does not talk about mysticism but
about sex appeal, the enraptured poet-reporter is reminded by a
script girl. (p. 175) Beyond its apparent extravagance, such a scene
projects the "real" perception of Cendrars in this world of "fac-
toried" imagination. For him, the only valid laboratory of magic is in
the mind of the writer who can create as many "true" worlds with
only pen and paper. Hence, when dealing with a world of manufac-
tured fancy, Cendrars's canon of journalistic accuracy was to manufacture a fanciful reportage.

III   *The War Reportings*

After these first two reporting assignments, Cendrars left journalism to return to his own style of nonfiction writing: short stories,
presumably based on real people he had known. He will, however,
come back to the field at the beginning of the Second World War
when, as war correspondent attached to British Headquarters in
France, he wrote a series of articles on the British army for several
French provincial newspapers,[6] which he collected in the volume
Chez l'armée anglaise.

Apparently Cendrars took his new function very seriously. His friend Nino Frank even recalled with some humor how, once he had donned the British War Correspondent's uniform, he took on the "look of an old colonel" and "seemed rather conceited about the importance of his position" (vol. 8, p. XIII). This new task was indeed of a more purely professional character, but it left very little leeway for the writer's imaginative talent.

The volume is cast in the personal tone of the previous reportings insofar as each piece revolves around Cendrars's presence and resorts to anecdotes unexpected in a routinely dry, clearcut war chronicle. Visiting the British army base in Western France, Cendrars reports more on the courtesy of a young colonel and the quality of the bar and top rate restaurant created by a Scottish major than on military activities. The highlights of a ten-day trip through England are the witty conversations of the eight journalists travelling together and the feats of the driver who conducts their bus with zest and whimsy along the icy roads. A cannon factory, a bomber's construction plant, a submarine base visited on the way are dutifully described. A day on the Northern Sea on board a destroyer escort is clearly of greater interest to the reporter and provides a more dynamic chapter. There is no doubt that for this war correspondent carrying out the officially assigned functions has less appeal than storing up impressions of the country and its people. His reporting only comes truly alive when, taking a day off to see the "man on the street," he visits the London docks. In fact the mechanized aspects of modern war methods only arouse Cendrars's melancholy and nostalgia for the oldtime tradition of the days of cavalry or the one-to-one encounters with the enemy he had known in 1914 in the Legion. After his visit to Sandhurst, he cannot help commenting:

There are millions of other small scientific gadgets . . . each one more ingenious and more fun than the next, but whatever interest, diversion or feeling of wonder I would derive from them . . . none of them could make me forget the impression of melancholy I had as I visited Sandhurst, I the poet who first sang the modern world, I the least academic of men. (vol. 8, pp. 183–84)

The poet, indeed, had his own war to write about. He did not need the external stimulus of reporting to find material for his creative urge. He needed only to let his past life "spin at full speed like an old spliced film" (vol. 6, p. 142) to bring the reality of war back to his readers with all its poignancy in the series of recollections of self and others that constitute his later writing style from *Histoires Vraies* to *Le lotissement du ciel*.

CHAPTER 7

The Thousand and One Nights *of a Contemporary Writer*

As far as I am concerned, I must see things with my own eyes, touch them with my own fingers in order to love them and understand them, become one with them in my thoughts and reinvent them to animate them and make them live and live again. (vol. 9, p. 301)

THIS statement of Blaise Cendrars in *L'homme foudroyé* could almost sum up the process of absorption and transmutation of reality that characterizes the new mode of writing he adopted in 1937 with *Histoires Vraies* and refined through the four volumes of the tetralogy (*L'Homme foudroyé*, 1945; *La Main coupée*, 1946; *Bourlinguer*, 1948; *Le lotissement du ciel*, 1949). Cendrars's own differentiation between his "true stories" (*Histoires Vraies*, 1937; *La vie dangereuse*, 1938; *D'oultremer à indigo*, 1940) and his autobiographical writings of the tetralogy, reinforced by the chronological factor of five years of silence between the two series have led most critics to treat them separately. They differ indeed in degree of complexity of structure and style but not in kind.

The former are presented by the author as nonfiction stories, stories of real events *he* had witnessed, of people *he* had known, of places *he* had been to. But they are not intended to have an autobiographical function. Cendrars's "nominal presence" is meant to "warrant the authenticity of [his] story" as he put it in the first page of *D'oultremer à indigo*. This presence is not a unifying factor; each chapter constitutes a distinct self-contained short story. The four volumes of the tetralogy, on the other hand, are an indissoluble continuum of reminiscences of people, places, readings, personal adventures lived or dreamt about, cross references to previous writings, reflexive pauses on the nature of writing or the directions the world and man are taking today, spiritual meditations, all woven into an intricate web through the consciousness of the author. The

113

pervasive presence of the self as a unifying factor does not, however, establish these works as an autobiographical document in the traditional sense of the word. Nino Frank's approach to the tetralogy as an "autobiographical saga"[1] has already been qualified or discarded by recent studies of Jay Bochner, Yvette Bozon Scalzitti, and Jean Carlo Fluckiger who have demonstrated that the unravelling of truth and fiction in these narratives is superfluous since they are essentially the author's greatest tribute to the imaginative power of creative writing. Cendrars himself had invited such a reading in his numerous allusions to Schopenhauer's formula, "the world is my representation" and Gerard de Nerval's assertion *"Je est un autre."* In his own more concrete manner, he had clearly described his unique merging of inner and outer reality into a personal mythopoetic vision in evoking how he used to dream for hours crouched behind a lookout slit during the war:

My lookout slit, my mind was its shutter. My heart fastened on it as a lens. . . . The universe came to inscribe itself in my lookout slit equipped with a shutter: myself! . . . (vol. 12, p. 221)

Thus the world brought to life under Cendrars's pen is the one perceived through the camera eye of his mind and heart. The "true stories" are not any truer than the blend of myth and reality woven through the tetralogy. They both, in fact, constitute so many tales of the world as apprehended by Cendrars. Some originated from real experience ("things seen through [his] own eyes and touched with [his] own fingers") such as the war, Brazil, some people he actually met and books he read. Others were elaborated in the "dark chamber of his imagination." (vol. 12, p. 250) As will be seen in the following analysis they were all "reinvented to animate and make live and relive" the vertigo of the writer seized by an antinomian sense of magic and horror of being in the world and consumed by the compulsive urge to keep it alive through writing.

I *War: The Experience of an Ignominious Pandemonium*

The often quoted line of Apollinaire, "Ah! how beautiful is war"[2] was simply an aberration for Cendrars who still wondered in 1949 "how Apollinaire could have written such beautiful poems one night at the front, or in May, in June 1940, Aragon, who was also inspired by the war." (vol. 12, p. 204) War is not a place to hold a pen but to fire a gun, as he contemptuously informs a seedy secret police character in *La main coupée.* (vol. 10, p. 254)

The excruciating experience of the reality of war for Cendrars overrode constructions of the imagination. Although war held an important place in Dan Yack's *Confessions,* it still remained a literary abstraction. One had to wait until *"L'égoutier de Londres"* in *Histoires Vraies* and *"J'ai saigné"* in *La vie dangereuse* to read Cendrars's acknowledged evocations of his experience in the Foreign Legion. Even then, he remains comparatively reserved. The atrociously slow agony of Griffith, the London sewerman, is muted by the Alibaba like tale of his discovery of an entrance to the Bank of England's vault through the sewers. In *"J'ai saigné"* Cendrars swiftly passes over his evacuation to an army hospital after his amputation (the intended topic announced by the title) and diverts the reader's attention from himself to the horrendous butchering of a young roommate by the doctors. In fact the central focus of the story is the dedication of the nurse Adrienne whose strength is a foil to the experience of horror intimated by the author.

It is characteristic that, however powerful they are, these two stories are the only ones dealing with the war in the three volumes of "true stories." Cendrars was still holding back the truth about his war. "I could not find my words" he states disarmingly in the last volume of the tetralogy after questioning the function of a poet's consciousness at the front: "A witnessing eye? an indicting awareness? an automaton?" Yet "one is not neutral. . . . Silence is not human," as he says at the end of the same paragraph. (vol. 12, p. 204)

He will indeed break his silence. When he picks up his pen again in the solitude of his Aix-en-Provence retreat in 1943, the initial creative impulse is brought about by the memory of one night: "the most terrible one [he] ever lived, alone, at the front in 1915." (vol. 9, p. 43) War reminiscences are not only the triggering force of *L'Homme foudroyé.* They are the subject matter of an entire volume, *La Main coupée* and are closely woven into the fiber of *Lotissement du ciel* as an unexpected catalytic agent of the author's visionary flights of imagination.

With all his natural tendency towards hyperbole, Cendrars's war stories are probably the most moving and true-to-life texts ever written on the reigning spirit of the trenches during World War I.

There is of course a share of gasconade in the account of the pranks
he played against the sergeants, his impudence towards upper-
ranking officers, his selfless dedication in helping his comrades get a
Croix de Guerre (while he himself constantly refuses decorations
and promotions), his being the best shot, the most alert patrolman.
There is also an element of extravagant overstatement in several
hair-raising descriptions such as the one concerning the glutton
Rossi who isolates himself in a shelter infested with the stench of
excrement and corpses to stuff himself with food parcels sent by his
wife but then is disembowelled into his tin plate when a bombshell
strikes him as he feasts on his spoils. Similarly a hilarious passage on
the regiment's motley clothing resulting from chaotic counter orders
from the administration is not without literary complacency. But the
spirit of tall stories was inherent to the rank and file army life,
especially in the Legion and even Cendrars's exaggerations contrib-
ute to the re-creation of a throbbingly real atmosphere.

In fact most of the obviously fabulated elements are in keeping
with the tradition of wry humor characteristic of the soldiers' morale
in the trenches. When a comrade is blown to smithereens by a
bombshell the shock is disguised by a cool comment such as: "One
less to be buried." The bloodcurdling story of Garnero who was
buried alive after his mates found him with his skullcap on his face
and thought him dead, but was "fortunately" catapulted out of his
burial hole by another bombshell which blew his leg off and brought
him back to life, is counterbalanced by stories of all the good meals
he used to prepare for the unit. In another instance, a Rabelaisian
mock epic of three hundred horses brought to Paris as a gift to
France by a Canadian rancher and the Gogolian tribulations undergone by their donor in the various Paris war offices serve as a comic
relief to ward off the emotion of Cendrars's previous comments on
the true love for France—not mercenary interest—which prompted
hundreds of foreigners to volunteer for the war.

In these war memories Cendrars's mythopoetic talents are possibly put to their best use: in the revelation of the undisguised truth
about one of the most commonly mythified topics. Through his
consummate balancing of all shades of humor (broad, wry, tender,
malicious, bitter, salacious) and Gothic horror, he probably
achieved the most candid iconoclastic portrayal of the colossal
absurdity that war actually is.

Mocking the conventional "literary" view of war embodied by the
secondrate poet-secret police agent who is exhilarated by the "sub-

lime," the "heroic," the "unexpected," the "picturesque" of life in the trenches, Cendrars answers:

> War is trash . . .
> Do you think you are in the theatre, Sir? . . .
> War is ignominious. (vol. 10, pp. 253, 254)

In an earlier passage he expresses the same disgust:

I hasten to say that war is not beautiful . . . from all the battles I have been in I have brought back nothing but an image of pandemonium. I wonder where they get their ideas when guys say they have lived historical or sublime hours. (vol. 10, p. 59)

That very ignominious pandemonium is what Cendrars actually depicted. The first chapter of *L'Homme foudroyé* in which he briefly evokes all the lost friends whose stories will constitute the chronicle of *La Main coupée* does not extoll heroism of any kind but describes the "degrading" fear which gripped them all including himself and the "moral depravation" brought about by "the miseries of the first world war." None of the deaths described in *La Main coupée* is the result of heroic battles. Rossi's example given above is but one among many other degradingly absurd deaths or mutilations which strike: Garnero while stealing a beer keg, Lang while going on leave, others, mutilating themselves on purpose in order to be evacuated, etc. Decorations are given arbitrarily for ridiculous reasons such as with Sawo, who got the *Croix de Guerre* for bringing a German machinegun he had stolen from a dead enemy. Another target of his scathing raillery is the inefficiency of the upper military command. Generals do not know what to do with a prisoner whose capture, incidentally, was not a heroic act, since he was deserting. Refusing the gift of a clay pipe from a general is considered an "insult to superiors" and is punished with a hundred days of prison.

The poet hardly needs to resort to his hyperbolic imagination. Shattered by the overwhelming reality of such a spectacle of human waste, he is left wordless with nothing but death in the soul. This is best expressed by the following passage from *Lotissement du ciel:*

The agony of life, the anonymous suffering multiplied by as many figures as they were in the regimental numbers of millions and millions of soldiers on the fire line, generations of living dead on the no man's land border, is it possible to conceive of a more absurd and more logical synthetic picture of this huge nonsense that human life on earth really is, a better illustration of the nothingness of man's spiritual life, a more patent proof of the power-lessness, the uselessness of his intellectual activity? There was no name for it. . . . (vol. 12, p. 202)

Mythopoetic imagination, on the contrary, becomes the only re-vitalizing force to pull him out of the sordid absurdity of self-destructive mankind. "Not to scream day and night, I keep telling myself negro stories" confessed Cendrars (vol. 12, p. 242). In the same volume, contemplating the sky while bombshells pour like hail around him, mythological tales of Lemurian tribes nourish his reverie and lead to a wealth of visions that fill the pages of his text. The unspeakable reality of war may very well be one of the decisive factors which led Cendrars to take refuge in the inner realm of fantasy and create the mythic vision of the world that constitutes many of his other stories.

II   *Brazil, a Conjurer's Hat or a Pandora Box*

The sponsoring of three prolonged visits to Brazil by the Sao Paulo coffee magnate and bibliophile, Paulo Prado, between 1924 and 1928, could not have happened at a more opportune time. It undoubtedly revitalized the restless writer, embittered and disheart-ened as he was by the directions he envisaged for man's future in Europe. Twice in the tetralogy Cendrars refers to his departures for Brazil as an antidote to the despair encroaching upon him:

. . . between 1924 and 1936, not a year went by without my spending one, three, nine months in America, especially in South America (when others went to Moscow), so weary was I of old Europe, despairing of its future and of the white race

he wrote in *L'Homme foudroyé* (vol. 9, p. 310). In *Le lotissement du ciel,* after a long digression on the materialism of the contemporary world, the misuse of reason, the cataclysmic trends of Western civilization in which wars, technology, and political strife were leading to the "decadence of the human species," he expresses again the same feelings toward his experience of Brazil:

And it may be why, sensing all this was coming, I went away and roamed about Brazil as early as 1924. . . . (vol. 12, p. 178)

With its vast unexplored expanses of undeveloped lands juxtaposed with supermodern highrise cities, its crucible of cultures
and races in which ancient practice of primitive magic coexists with
sophisticated Western rationalism, a boisterous dynamism and constant movement together with an undercurrent of fatalism and
passive abandon to the lulling effects of the tropics, the reality of
Brazil was equal to the measure of Cendrars's imagination. It
provided him with a wealth of hyperbolic visions, simultaneous
contrasts, living myths that had always inhabited the poet's mind.

The Brazil-inspired texts, which constitute the majority of the
cycle of "true stories," are interspersed in several chapters of
L'Homme foudroyé and become the backbone of the last section of
Le lotissement du ciel. They convey at first the author's enthusiasm
for this country of "an unspeakable grandeur" which "takes your
breath away with admiration and often with terror or passion." (vol.
15, p. 27) They also give the impression that Brazil (at times
extended to other South American countries) had become for Cendrars his magician's hat out of which he pulled at will an assortment
of extravagant creatures and situations in order to titillate the jaded
European reader's interest.

The relentless life of diamond seekers in the Matto Grosso *("Le
cercle du diamant");* miracles performed by a halfwit sexton in
Santiago do Chili *("Le Saint inconnu");* the beauty of the Amazonian
jungle *("En transatlantique dans la forêt vierge");* Christmas cele-
bration in Bahia ("Febronio"); the burlesque pranks in Paris of an
uncouth *fazenda* manager who, sitting naked at his hotel window,
throws orange peels on the Place de l'Opéra and still naked hangs
out of his balcony railing to see what is attracting the crowd gathered
by his antics *("Coronel Bento");* mock heroic stories of tiger, boas
and crocodile hunting; a boa which starves itself in order to escape
through the bars of a cage where he is kept on a fazenda *("Mes
chasses");* black women sitting on a red sofa in the middle of the
jungle while they wait for the road to be built; or a piano being
carried on foot over the Andes for a man who has never seen a piano
but ordered it to cure his wife's melancholy *(L'Homme foudroyé);*
Cendrars's own extravagances when sailing back to Europe with
sixty-seven monkeys and two hundred and fifty septicolor
birds. . . . All these and many more such anecdotes in which
Cendrars gave a free rein to his story telling fantasy elaborate a truly
Cendrarian mythology of Brazil.

At the same time, however, Brazil seems to have opened a Pandora's box for Cendrars. Beneath their surface exuberance most of his Brazilian stories are steeped in violence, death, desolation of the land and the sense of incongruity of man's presence on it.

In *"Le cercle du diamant"* for instance, behind the glitter of Edith de Berensdoff's most exclusive nightclub in Rio de Janeiro lurks human tragedy. She had really opened the club, where it was customary to pay for her favor with diamonds, because she wanted them for her husband, to compensate him upon his return from a fruitless search for the blue diamond in the Matto Grosso. Her secret is discovered when she falls unconscious one night, stricken by the telepathic knowledge of her husband's death. He had actually been shot and killed in the diamond seekers' camp on that night. Cendrars packs into the vivid tale the picturesque and dramatic description of the diamond seekers' adventurous life, the contrasting artifice of the Rio de Janeiro night life, the destructiveness of the lure of fortune and grippingly projects all the underlying pathos.

The story of Febronio is one of the most striking examples of Cendrars's perception of the darker side of things hidden under the shimmering surface of Brazil. Febronio, a psychically deranged black Brazilian convinced he had a divine mission to kill the demon, actually existed. Very much like the recently convicted "Son of Sam" in New York, he had "sacrificed" scores of young men in Rio a few years before Cendrars's visit.[3] Cendrars's encounter with Febronio in the Rio prison serves as a springboard not only to the bloodcurdling life scenario of this "illuminated" killer. Other such examples of murders due to mental derangements are also given, such as the one of Kadota, the successful Japanese gardener in Sao Paulo who, one night, killed his entire family as a sacrifice to his ancestral gods. This leads Cendrars to a serious consideration of the problems raised by the inhibiting factor inherent in the clash between modern civilization and the spirituality of primitive magic.

Violent deaths due to the imbalance between man and his environment are a recurrent theme. The jovial, swaggering *Coronel* Bento who, besides fathering about fifty children on the *fazenda* he manages, prides himself on his art of roping horses, was maimed and left with a scar that encircled his entire body after an unsuccessful attempt to catch and kill the werewolf. He dies much later, the victim of his own pride and excessive confidence when, dragged by a wild mare he defiantly insists on catching, his scar reopens and he bleeds to death. Another example of violent deaths caused by the excess to which humans are driven in that land where the mysterious and the fantastic reign supreme, is that of Logrado. Crazed by his hunting feats he decides to attack a thousand-year-old boa, "the king of the country," and is drowned when his frightened horse races across the river and gets caught in an old fence.

When death and violence are not the outcome of Cendrars's stories, the underlying tone is that of the soul-destroying loneliness of man, the waste of his efforts against the all-powerful jungle, an overall atmosphere of desolation. Joao do Barros (the German diamond seeker), Febronio, Dakota, Logrado, Bento, whether real or imaginary characters are all deeply solitary beings. So are less tragic protagonists. Manolo Secca, the owner of the last gas station on a deserted road of the Matto Grosso finds compensation in carving a Way of the Cross. Since hardly any car ever comes through he carves each sculpture to represent a figure standing in an automobile *("Le chemin brulé)*. Pierre le Métis, the snake hunter, attempts to escape his loneliness with dreams of "all the lovely little feet on the London or Paris pavements" to the beauty of which he contributes with his snake skins. He has also built himself a radio set and lucidly acknowledges:

It is a good thing I have a degree in engineering because I was starting to be eaten up by nostalgia. (vol. 9, p. 317)

The pervasive sadness which lies in wait for every individual is stirringly evoked in the story of Padroso in *"La Tour Eiffel sidérale."* Morro Azul, a sumptuous colonial plantation, originally built for the Emperor Don Pedro, is an apt setting for the life of unrealized dreams of his owner Padroso. In a previous story, Cendrars had already suggestively described the desolation and waste on an abandoned plantation: Dona Viridiana's estate in which "not only the fazenda was antique, the house dry rotting, men old, but the earth itself no longer fertile." (vol. 8, p. 266) Morro Azul conveys the same feeling of organic exhaustion and decay to the visitor. It is also drenched with eeriness. Its atmosphere is that of a haunted castle in a Gothic tale: a female snake sleeps in a net hung over the bed in the master bedroom, huge spiders come out of the pool's pipes, the land is an overgrown waste. In that land where "everything grows with exaggeration, feelings as much as hostile nature" (vol. 12, p. 169), Padroso lives like a hermit lost in his love for the actress Sarah Bernhardt to whom, for twenty years, he had been writing letters he locks in a safe. His passion for Sarah Bernhardt, which stirred an equally fanatic passion for France, had led the poor man to a vision of a new constellation in the sky in the shape of the Eiffel Tower. The hope of having his discovery scientifically acknowledged by the Institute of Astronomy is probably the only sustaining power in the life of this rich but desperately solitary *fazenda* owner.

Cendrars's portrayal of Brazil is double-edged.[4] Beneath the glamour of the exhilaration of adventure, freedom, and exoticism, there is a deep layer of human realism, which, as is frequently the case in his writings, Cendrars dissimulates behind a screen of fanciful boisterous invention. His knowledge of Brazil may not be dissimilar to the ideal knowledge of France that Padroso had:

An ideal knowledge . . . made of nostalgia and crude details picked up here and there, vertiginously true and irreal or surreal as all that comes to us through imagination or reading or by abstraction, deduction, study, cross-checking. . . . (vol. 12, p. 297)

Nevertheless the fact that he never went to the Amazon or to the Matto Grosso, that the largest tree he ever saw was a fig tree in the Sao Paulo garden of Dona Olivia Guedes de Penteado,[5] that some characters are real like Febronio, that others have been recreated from original types and others purely invented, in no way alters or diminishes the essence of Brazil captured in his visionary blend of fact and fiction.[6]

Cendrars's imaginative genius had responded to the Brazil in which "the pictorial consumes the imagination; leaf and scrub, seaside and backlands long for their apotheosis as word," as Elizabeth Hardwick put it in her article "Sad Brazil."[7] But like the British writer and, before her, Levi-Strauss in *Sad Tropics*, he himself had captured the inner core of sadness in that:

seductive country, all in simultaneous contrasts and what dangerous ones, as it appears in unanimous statements made by Brazilians, these feverishly talkative people whose verbalism hides the deep melancholy to which man becomes a prey in this torrid climate, feeling lost in this immense country and immensely powerless and useless in front of the immensity of his task, and, in spite of the stimulating force of his most exalting successes which he knows to be artificial, from generation to generation he falls back into a sickly nonchalance, a discouraged fatigue. . . . (vol. 12, p. 170)

Cendrars's love for Brazil was genuine and there is no exaggeration in his statement in *Trop c'est trop* that he "considers Brazil his second spiritual fatherland." (vol. 15, p. 105) His passion for the country and its people was such, in fact, that his influence in the Modernist circles of Sao Paulo writers was to revive their interest in their own national culture (a spirit underlying the Pau Brazil movement of 1925) rather than encourage them in their Paris-imported modernity.[8] Yet, just as he discerned a deep melancholy concealed by the feverish verbalism of the Brazilians there also lurked, beneath the exuberance of his evocations of Brazil, a foreboding reality. The conjurer's skill did not succeed—and maybe did not intend—to seal Pandora's box.

III   *Through the Kaleidoscope of Memories and Fantasies:*
Recapturing the Magic of Life or Exorcising Visions of Darkness

Cendrars's exaltation over what he called the "profound today" and his well known lyricism about speed, movement, trains, cars, his fascination with dictaphones and cameras must not mislead the reader into seeing him as an epigone of the Futurists, an unquestioning supporter of modernity. His works, on the contrary, are pervaded by his pessimistic comments on the contemporary world, its mechanization, robotization of thought, its loss of magic and sense of wonder. Against this background, the vertiginous maze of themes, characters, anecdotes, events, legends, philosophical comments which, in addition to the war and Brazilian stories, rush on in a torrential flow through the pages of these seven volumes, appears as a rescue operation. The writer seems to have undertaken to bring out of this dulled modern world all possible elements of magic, marvelous or bizarre, as thrilling as those of ancient tales or Gothic horror stories.

Adventures on ocean liners, freighters or small coasters; elephant hunting in Africa; gargantuan meals in fishermen pubs; ribaldry in drug dens; wild love nights; spells of visionary trance; encounters with weird witchlike women, lepers, bums of all sorts, freaks, publicly known characters including writers and artists; gypsy vendettas, the ghoulish account of the monstrous cloning of human beings experimented on by eighteenth-century black magic practitioners. . . . These are but a few items featured in these kaleidoscopic narratives. The proliferation of subject matter is only matched by the irrepressible exuberance of the prose which captures the simultaneity of perception in the vortex of multiplicity through sentences three- or four-pages-long in a neoBaroque blend of ingenious structural calculation and flamboyant profusion. Any attempt at summarizing any of these chapters would result in a dizzying inventory which would obliterate the life of the kind of organic growth these writings are.

Common to all these variegated stories or tales is a polarization of perception similar to the one illustrated by the Brazilian episodes: an exalted sense of the wonder of life in its dynamism and eccentricity constantly pitted against a baleful view of existence expressed in violent deaths, mutilations, an inexhaustible variety of physical and spiritual sufferings.

With all the joviality and good spirits of hard drinking and hard working life on board a freighter, "T.P.M.T.R." is a model of macabre humor. The title means "you leave but you will come back," the acronym of the French "Tu Pars Mais Tu Reviendras," the name of a sailors' association which ensures the return of its members' dead bodies. For that purpose a very ornate coffin is kept on board. The action pivots around the cook's death, the swelling of his corpse in the coffin, which the captain is finally obliged to have thrown overboard, and the coffin's reappearance off the Florida coast, looked upon by the exhilarated crew as an act of magic.

Unexpected deaths bring to an end the most spirited evocations of the fullness of life. The jolly Montparnasse tramp-turned-ambassador succumbs to a heart attack soon after occupying his position ("S. E. l'Ambassadeur"), Jicky, the solid country boy evoked several times as Cendrars's cameraman in his fantasized filmmaking expeditions, dies a drug addict in a Marseilles hospital (L'Homme foudroyé). Beatrix, the heroine of "La femme aimée," is killed in a plane accident on the eve of her uniting happiness in love with professional success as a singer in her lover's operatic production. The fairy land atmosphere of Paquita's ultra rich "chateau" is marred by the spiritual decay of this beautiful and intelligent multimillionaire woman who commits suicide after giving all her fortune to the Mexican Revolution (L'Homme foudroyé). The accidental shooting by hunters of Cendrars's little girlfriend, Elena, in "Gênes" (Bourlinguer) brings to an end the evocation of the innocent playfulness of his early childhood in Naples, and leads to gruesome tales of sorcery which allegedly took place in Virgil's accursed grave enclosure (his and Elena's former playground). As if the account of these past maledictions did not suffice, Cendrars updates the myth with the haunting story of his killing a monstrously defaced leper. The leper in question is none other than the sorcerer Monsignore, father of Il Dommatore, an even more grisly character who used to burn stolen children to shrink them into dwarfs and make them perform in the streets to the tune of his barbary organ!

Weird or mutilated characters are not exceptions in Cendrars's world and are often complacently described at length. The two most striking ones are Marthe, Gustave Lerouge's wife, disfigured by an ulcerous slash across her face (*L'Homme foudroyé*) and Felicia, the heroine of "*l'Amiral*," another of these multimillionaire women of extraordinary beauty, who has been left after a car accident with her face split by a scar from the root of the hair to the chin. Before her lover, Jensen, the handsome captain of a Danish transatlantic liner makes up his mind to divorce his wife and marry her, Felicia lives on board disguised as Feli, Jensen's Malaysian private manservant. This human tragedy, which ends with the moral and spiritual disintegration of them both following their marriage and retirement to a Montevideo residence, is narrated against the background of the brilliant jet-set life aboard the liner, the grandeur of South American coast lines, Cendrars's own boisterousness and pranks, such as his bringing a goat on deck to throw to the sharks. The extravagant goat story itself follows the same dualistic pattern since the gratuitous cruelty inflicted on the poor animal ends up in laughter with the sharks frightened and the goat swimming back to the coast. The scene is summed up with the humorous rhymed couplet:

> Que pensez vous qu'il arriva
> Ce fut le bouc qui surnagea
> (What do you think happened, It was the goat that surfaced)
> (vol. 8, p. 317)

In a similar vein, the idyllic retreat of La Redonne in "*Le vieux port*" (*L'Homme foudroyé*) is made uneasy by the haunting presence of the witchlike halfwit "*Femme à Mick.*" In the same chapter, the cordial atmosphere of the fishermen's café "Chez Felix," where

Cendrars describes with a Rabelaisian verve his evenings of merry eating and drinking, is tarnished by another feature: Felix's wife, the cook, is dumb, having had her tongue cut off in a car accident.

Cendrars's obsession with the unwonted, the bizarre, violence and cruelty finds unlimited space in the evocation of the Gypsy world which constitutes the framework of "*Rhapsodies Gitanes*," the second part of *L'Homme foudroyé*. An obvious symbol for a life of untrammelled freedom, the gypsies are used as an archetypal foil to other episodes signalling within the narration a need for escape from constraints: Gustave Lerouge's withdrawal from society in the elaboration of his fabulous three hundred and fifty popular thrillers; Paquita's refuge into the mysteries of the Mayan alphabet; Cendrars's own flight outward along his mythic National 10 highway which goes from the Paris suburbs to Paraguay. In fact the most colorful and picturesque piece in the Gypsy cycle is the portrayal of "*Le Père Francois*," a stereotypical old tinker, a master in the art of whip wielding, who roams through the gypsy zone with his battered cart and rules tyrant-like over his shanty town of cut throats called the "*caravane-misère*." But "*Le Père Francois*" is only a tramp figure peripheral to the gypsy world to which he does not belong by blood. Behind the aura of mystery and romance that Cendrars lends to the Gypsies there is strong emphasis on the relentlessly rigorous inner laws of cruelty and violence that bind them all. The vendettas between kings of different tribes are not vaudeville stagesettings. The barbarous training of children whether to beg, rob, or perform circus acrobatics is dramatically projected. Even when in "*Les Ours*" Cendrars relates the plot of a theatrical show performed by "*Le Grêlé's*" itinerant company, he selects a Surrealistic blood-curdling werewolf story of merciless killings and tortures. In the world of the Gypsies, artists of illusion, Cendrars's predilection for the dark side of things hidden behind a glittering surface finds the perfect habitat.

Such constant recurrence of this dualistic pattern evokes the image of the writer as a modern version of the court jester. The image is, in fact, suggested by Cendrars himself when, reminiscing in *Bourlinguer* of his readings of the fourth-century monk Cassien, he pretends to recognize his double in one of his pages:

And at the turn of a page, here is my portrait as if photographed by a photomaton. . . . "We have found other demons. . . . There are in fact among them what the vulgar calls the Wanderers—Planos—who are above all seducers and jesters. . . ." I knock myself against the mirror. (vol. 11, pp. 83–84)

The portrait is complete: deviltry, seduction, and buffoonery. The deviltry and seduction are inherent to the unabashed mythmaking that characterizes all Cendrars's writings. Of the jester what these stories reflect is mostly the pervasive sense of sadness and suffering hidden by the boisterous extravagance of the storytelling. Whether in luminous tales of adventure or somber tales of horror this kaleidoscopic mythopoetic construct appears as the writer's antidote to, and exorcism of, a haunting vision of darkness.

IV *The Writer's Saga*

The unifying element throughout this complex web of stories is the author, not only nominally present as a narrator and witness of the events, but as an active participant and subject/object of the narration. A polarization, similar to that analyzed in the preceding sections, but even further amplified affects the projection of the self, whose deeper inner truth is willfully obscured behind the elaborate construct of a persona of mythic stature.

A biographer of Cendrars who would use these volumes as a main source of documentation would be victim of the same lure and experience the same disappointment as the blue diamond seekers of the Rio dos Garcias in Cendrars's story *"Le cercle du diamant."* Some rare revelations of the authentic Cendrars glitter like raw diamonds at the bottom of the muddy torrentuous stream of his narrative flow, but they slip out of reach carried away by the strength of the current the moment one lays a hand on them. At the same time, Cendrars has laid out for his reader a well displayed series of meticulously carved false stones that have a most attractive shine. Three rather moving allusions to his love for Raymone, for instance, are inserted in *L'Homme foudroyé.* They are sufficiently powerful to throw light on one of the meanings of the title: *"foudroyé,"* literally thunderstruck, means here blasted by bombshells as much as stricken by lightning through love and, as will be seen later, stricken by visionary illumination. Such allusions are not dwelled upon, they are immediately absorbed into extravagant stories of Gypsies or hunting or speeding on the roads. Some of these "blue diamonds" have sent researchers on valid tracks such as Cendrars's admission to his pilfering from Lerouge's novels which led Francis Lacassin to his discovery.[9] Most of the writer's sources in fact are almost candidly disclosed throughout his texts: Baudelaire, Goethe, Nerval, Schopenhauer, Nietzsche, Remy de Gourmont as well as less obvious ones such as an anonymous Brazilian almanac which "made [him] enter deeper into the soul of Brazil than any other publication by a member of the Brazilian Academy. . . ." (vol. 9, p. 350) Similarly, several places and people described were active components of his life: for example, La Pierre where he wrote *L'Eubage*, La Redonne, his country house in Le Tremblay, Brazilian plantations, Paulo Prado, writers and artists— among them Delaunay, Cravan, Léger, Apollinaire, André Gaillard, Cocteau, Radiguet, Reverdy. But for each true fact of his life the reader will find myriad additional fabulations: the shooting of documentary films on elephants in Africa, on boas in Brazil, the tiger hunts and horseback riding, the driving of torpedoes through the South American jungle or tractors in Winnipeg, killing the leper in Naples, and many such feats which have contributed to build the well-known legendary image of Cendrars.

This blend of partial confessions and mythmaking bravado is not meant, however, to mystify the reader. Cendrars's fascination with the workings of imagination is clear. The first section of *"Le vieux port"* in *L'Homme foudroyé* entitled *"Festival de l'Invention"* un-equivocally places his narrative under the auspices of the mystic's seizure of the "signature of things" and ends with the all-too-transparent allusions to Goethe's *Dichtung und Wahrheit* and Gérard de Nerval's *Le rêve et la vie* [*Poetry and truth/dream and life*]. In the last volume, *Le lotissement du ciel*, when a third revised version of his favorite tale of personal adventure, his transSiberian trip with the jewel smuggler Rogovine is offered (but this time with a few hints at real facts),[10] it appears with the title: "The Dark Chamber of Imagination." The actual existence of the dark room in which he used to sort out precious stones does not obliterate its symbolical meaning. The mythopoetic intent is openly avowed.

The object of Cendrars's mystification is less the reader than the self whose true essence, an abysmal inner void, is skillfully evaded through this polymorphous imaginative construct. That self, however, is not Cendrars's own ego, but the writer's self caught in the cycle of the wheel of things and tortured by the incompleteness of creativity.

The substratum of *L'Homme foudroyé* is indeed the consumma-tion of the writer in his solitude as if struck by lightning from his exposure to the "secret of things" (vol. 9, p. 192). The solitude of the writer, repeatedly expressed throughout this volume, is not the escape from the madding crowd sought in various retreats as La Pierre, La Redonne or La cornue. It is a spiritual solitude that estranges the writer and leads to silence in the contemplation of the whole, the absolute irreducible Word: "One is in an integral solitude. . . . And one keeps silent in one's yearning for the Word." (vol. 9, p. 192)

Writing thus becomes a demoniac activity:

When the voice of God resounds through the desert, the Devil writes it . . . and boasts about it. (vol. 9, p. 353)

Cendrars states it at the end of the volume when tempted to write the story of Maripuru, a white man discovered by Pedro Alvarez Cabral when he landed in Santos in 1501.[11]

In this context Cendrars's fantasmagoric storytelling takes on a Dionysian character. As if compelled by the devil, the writer surrenders to an orgiastic need of creation which fills the inner void of the contemplative self. In many respects the space of Cendrars's imaginative representation may be compared to Paquita's chambers filled with dolls—re-creations of characters from novels or native types of her country—which she made to dispel her neurasthenia. There is in Cendrars's compulsive writing a form of despair reminiscent of the Dada spirit. Just as for Tzara's "Approximative Man," as Micheline Tison Braun perceptively pointed out, there is no escape from the void within.[12] It must be stoically faced. The only release from its unendurable pressure is the "explosion of life" in the high voltage climate of intense and incessant creation. The inescapability of writing and its anguishing inconclusiveness is clearly expressed in *Bourlinguer:*

One does not live in the absolute. . . . Life is not logic, the art of portrayal perspective, nor the creation of a writer a likeness. . . . We will never know any other traces of life—life of the planet—life of the individual—but what comes to consciousness in the form of writing (sous traces d'écriture). . . . Poetry. Hence creation. Hence action. And only action liberates. Otherwise there is a short circuit, the universe is set ablaze and everything falls back into the night of the spirit. (vol. 11, p. 322)

However protected it is by the smokescreen of fabulation, the writer's irresistible submission to the relativity of action (i.e., writing) as an antidote to the eclipse of the mind threatening the seeker for the absolute, is the underlying concern of the self projected in the last two volumes of the tetralogy: *Bourlinguer* and *Le lotissement du ciel.*

Bourlinguer, which literally means "roughing it" contains its due share of cock and bull stories. Its primary topic, nevertheless, is not the travel anecdotes which the names of European seaports as chapter headings might suggest. It is essentially the writer's *"bourlinguage"* through *"l'espace de l'écriture,"* his own and that of others. The tone is set in the first chapter, "Venise" which is about an ancient account of the discovery of India found in the Saint Marc library and the distortions made by Jesuit scholars in an originally authentic and picturesque narrative: natural creativity destroyed by erudition. The "sea port tour" ends in the last chapter with *"Paris port de mer"* which, among vignettes of various writers and book collectors Cendrars met in Paris libraries, focuses on reading and the reader's relationship to books, including Cendrars's own intoxication with reading, which is a mirrored refraction of his preoccupation with the function of writing. It is characteristic that what he admires most in assiduous readers is their ability to enter into a world of illusions; and that reading is compared to travel for its powers of displacement in space and time.

The core text in *Bourlinguer* is *"Gênes,"* a chapter which alone covers one hundred and fifty pages out of three hundred and fifty. The most intricate narrative network in Cendrars's entire production, *"Gênes"* interlocks almost all the themes of his repertoire like Chinese "hope-chest" boxes. Yet its substructure is strongly sustained by the search for the identity of the self.

The quest for the essence of being, which reenacts archetypal initiation rituals one after the other, is treated in a semi-burlesque manner. The return to the garden of childhood yields no illuminating memories. The experiment of entombment near Virgil's grave, inspired by Kim's example leads to the experience of nothingness. ("Either Kim's treatment is a joke or I do not have a sound mind, and the imitation of the tomb is hell." (vol. 11, p. 90) The systematic inventory of capital sins is no more enlightening. The "intermittent fire of consciousness" discovered in a meditation at the rudder of a boat at sea sends nothing but an undecipherable message. Regression to prenatal consciousness brings back a vision of the devil. Sailing aboard the Greek coaster (a rejuvenating cure after the entombment) is but a drinking brawl which ends in a whorehouse in

Genoa before the hero (Cendrars himself) jumps into a train for Paris, evoking the magnetic pole for all the Rastignacs of literature.

Behind this parodic treatment of the search for identity of self is hidden the writer's serious attempt to come to terms with the antinomies of the creative demoniac forces within him and "the contemplative person [he] never ceased to be." (vol. 11, p. 170) Once more writing is perceived as a decoy from the dread of the void within. While the performance he "executes in front of his typewriter" is compared to "the gymnastics and juggling" he used to practice to entertain the deck boy on board the Greek coaster (vol. 11, p. 167), the temptation of silence already present in *L'Homme foudroyé* recurs:

Why write, everything prints itself within me, and perhaps pure poetry is to let oneself be impregnated and decipher the signature of things within oneself. (vol. 11, p. 151)

Yet the Dionysian in Cendrars triumphs over the Apollonian. Just as in *L'Homme foudroyé* the "secret of things" had to be finally left to God's silence, the question "Who am I?" has to remain unanswered for the sake of the demon of creativity:

I do not have the time. . . . Life takes me away and writing is pressing me on. (vol. 11, p. 191)

In line with this pervasive awareness of the writer's inability to seize reality and turn language into logos, the mystical effusions of *Le lotissement du ciel* may be read as Cendrars's ultimate break-through into the ecstatic vision he had failed to experience in "*Gênes.*" It may also be understood as one of many instances of vicarious explorations originating in readings. But the very care with which Cendrars invites the reader to dissociate him from the relation of Saint John of Cupertino's and other saints' levitations, which constitute the first part of the volume, betrays the personal stake the writer had in this new venture. The topic of levitation is deferred twice by earthy stories: about his sailing from Brazil with two hundred and fifty birds (mentioned earlier) and about a cheerful dinner outing in Paris with his son and a lusty wench. His son, a war pilot, becomes one pretext for writing about the levitating saint who, according to Cendrars, should be the patron saint of aviation. Another is the Gestapo's spying on his comings and goings in Aix-en-Provence during World War II: Cendrars allegedly resumed his research on levitation at the Mejanes library of Aix to sidetrack the Gestapo. After all these unusual precautionary steps, Cendrars gingerly enters his new field of exploration through other mystical writings and scholarly works which he quotes at length.[13]

Only then does Cendrars unleash his visionary power and produce a text, *"le ravissement de l'amour,"* which may without exaggeration be considered Cendrars's literary levitation. In total empathy with the saint's ravishment, this section is a fireworks of lyrical esoteric poetic prose that stands comparison with Rimbaud's *Illuminations.* As Jay Bochner put it in his enlightening analysis of this volume, "the religious ecstacy completely submerges realistic narrative."[14]

Religious ecstasy, however, as was already intuited in the previous volumes, leads to silence, "a death to the world" which is untenable for the writer. Whether of a religious nature, as in the previous instance, or of a more secular character in *"La Tour Eiffel Sidérale,"* to cite the reverie brought about by the contemplation of the Coalsack or the lookout slit in the battlefield, every spiralling gyration of the writer's visionary flights brings him back, bitterly resigned, to the limitations of creative discourse.

The initial metaphor "writing is burning alive" which romantically started *L'Homme foudroyé* is replaced here by more sardonically realistic ones. The writer's task is compared to that of the underground miner who comes back to the surface unable to describe whatever findings he might have made but "speaks like a distracted man of the ghosts that appeared. . . ." (vol. 12, p. 244) The inner core of reality cannot be worded. Only visions and fabulations may be shaped by the creative discourse. Hence the reference on the same page to the writer as a master of artifice comparable to the scintillating shows of circus acrobats.

The relationship of the writing to life, that is of fiction to truth, now emerges in a very different light. The exuberance of mythopoetic liberties may be seen as the counterpart to the abyss of silence in which perception of the real plunges the mind. "Writing" truly becomes "an abdication" as Cendrars repeatedly stated, but not in the sense of a renunciation of life as it is commonly understood. The writer's abdication is on the contrary a surrender to relativity and multiplicity, a stoic acceptance to keep whirling on the wheel of things instead of coming to a standstill and silence in the contemplation of the One, the unspeakable.

As Jean Carlo Fluckiger noted:

One could consider [Cendrars's] entire work as a long figurative discussion on the impossibility to seize reality. At least from the philosophical point of view, this is the reason why he writes.[12]

The writer's saga woven through the intricate web of these tales of the self and others supports this interpretation. In the age of the "Literature of Exhaustion" and "The degree zero of writing" Cendrars had relived Rimbaud's temptation to withdraw into silence. But like the *Arabian Nights* storyteller, he chose to defy death and keep alive the smoldering embers of creativity.

CHAPTER 8

Literary Exorcism or Hedonism

W HEN Cendrars left his Villefranche retreat in 1950 to settle in Paris he came to the capital preceded by the aura of the legend created by his writings of the previous decade. Far from attempting to disclose his truer self, he seemed to have been more than willing to perpetuate the image of the world roamer the public so much enjoyed. Between October 15 and December 15, 1950, the French radio broadcast a series of interviews with the poet Robert Manoll in which Cendrars vehemently confirmed the truth of every one of his putative adventures, frequently embroidering the fictive canvas even more. The following year another series of radio broadcasts entertained the credulous public with Cendrars's Christmas stories from all over the world: *"Noëls du monde entier."* These interviews with Robert Manoll were subsequently published in *Blaise Cendrars vous parle* (1952) and the Christmas stories, originally published in the Parisian daily newspapers *Paris Presse* and *L'Intransigeant,* later became part of the collection of essays *Trop c'est Trop.*[1] During the first half of this decade the writer seems to have abandoned his fierce creative independence and through his popularity, succumbed to the temptation of occasional writing or commercial publications such as *Le Brésil, des hommes sont venus,* (an introduction to a photograph album on Brazil, which was mostly made up of previously published articles).

The demoniac creative fire was not extinct, however. In the 1950 radio interviews, complaining that readers saw nothing but himself in every one of his protagonists, Cendrars had announced in his tongue-in-cheek manner, that he was working on a "real novel" in which he himself would not appear:

I have a magnificent topic and this time it will be a real novel. . . . I will write a "roman-roman." (vol. 13, p. 57)

When the novel in question, *Emmène-moi au bout du monde,* came out six years later, it baffled, disappointed or outraged the critics who saw in it an awkward, even monstrous piece of writing, either a provocation from the notorious rebel or the embittered swan song of a declining creativity.

I *The Novel as a Vindictive Lampoon*

Cendrars kept his promise not to appear as a protagonist and to create a real novel—insofar as it is plotted around two major characters—an actress Thérèse, and her lover Jean, a legionnaire. The book, however, reads like a hodgepodge of pornography, teratology, crime, and scandal stories of all kinds.

Opening with the bombshell of a scabrous scene staging the copulating play between the lewd, purient, seventy-nine-year-old actress and the twenty-year-old, obscenely tattooed legionnaire who is brutishly pleasuring her in a dingy Paris hotel room reeking with the rancid putrefaction of fruit and vegetables in the nearby Halles, the narrative develops like an eschatological fireworks. Around Thérèse, who becomes the hit of the town by exhibiting her decaying bruised body on stage as she recites Villon's lament for vanished beauty at the end of the play *Madame L'Arsouille* in which she stars, Cendrars accumulates a gallery of moral and physical freaks. The choice pieces strain the limits of credibility: La Présidente, a trunk woman whose "beautiful woman's bust" incites a passionate lesbian love in Thérèse; Sam Bonfils, a tongueless black servant taking care of La Présidente with the help of peyote through which they discover "the magic art of living"; Emile, a blackmarketeering bistro owner who uses his Legion of Honor decoration to outwit the police in his countless fraudulent deals and arouses his mistresses by showing them a war wound (artificial intestines held in his side by a metal disc which he too willingly unscrews in public). The general social backdrop displays a galaxy of libidinous old wealthy gentlemen, homosexual artists and writers, corrupted chiefs of police, blackmarketeers, drug addicts, and spurious drama critics.

First centered on the specificity of the heroine's sexual and thespian feats, the action moves to yet another highly charged order of content. After a rehearsal had been broken up by a power failure the entire cast, who had settled down to a dinner in a restaurant near which a murder has just been committed, is taken to the police headquarters for interrogation. Cendrars uses this subplot to occasion a further flow of hairraising tales interwoven with scathingly satirical comments on Parisian society. The focus shifts back to the production of the play which Thérèse's "ultra realism" makes a record-breaking success. The narrative is brought to an end by the death of the heroine, which edges on the burlesque. Did Cendrars wish to nonplus the reader who might have expected the octogenarian actress to collapse at any moment from the physical and emotional stress of her sexual orgies and exhilarating stage success? Instead, Thérèse is stung by a bee while picking cherries, breaks her leg falling off the tree and dies not from the fall but from a general infection caused by the bee sting.

In spite of the lighthearted demise of the main character *Emmène moi au bout du monde* seems far from "the cheerful little novel" which Cendrars pretended to have written.[2] Teratological inspiration had been pervasive in many of Cendrars's writings, but here he outdoes Céline and Genêt and the authors of *Fantomas* combined. Profile upon profile of physical and moral aberrations stud the narrative to the point of parodic saturation. And this insistence on the grotesque and the macabre runs parallel to yet another overabundance of virulently acid diatribes that textures the monologues of each protagonist. The caricatural intensity of the satire obscures at first what the work is unto itself. It seems to be merely the objurgation of an embittered, aging writer spewing out his repressed wrath and slashing through the entire rotting fabric of a society he is rejecting.

The most immediate target of the attack is the Parisian world of the theater. Although in a prefatory note Cendrars begs the reader not to be inelegant enough to identify the characters of his novel, which he admits to be a *roman à clé*, most of them are easily recognized. The director of the theater company, Felix Juin is Louis Jouvet. The play *Madame l'Arsouille* is *La Folle de Chaillot* by Jean Giraudoux, known in the novel as Guy de Montauriol. The set designer Coco is in real life Christian Bérard and Thérèse's first husband, Maurice Strauss, is the writer Marcel Schwob. Thérèse herself is none other than the famous actress of the period Marguerite Moreno.[3] Cendrars had, of course, first-hand knowledge of Louis Jouvet's company since his wife, Raymone, had been acting in it for over thirty years. Yet, whatever personal vindication may be perceived in Cendrars's treatment of one of the most famous theater productions of the time, it does not constitute the main springboard of the narrative.

It contains another salient feature which acts as both index and agent to the revelation of the seethingly angry mood belaboring the author while he was writing the novel: the unrestrained display of erotic perversion. For the first time in Cendrars's work, sodomy as well as heterosexual libido are treated with open complacency, to such an extent that Yvette Bozon Scalzitti, in her recent analysis of the novel, felt entitled to see it as "the key . . . to the entire work of Cendrars, which in extremis he opens to its sexual truth, until then more or less masked or repressed."[4] The portrayal of the nymphomaniac, at times lesbian, indomitable actress may be interpreted as a scream of rage, a revolt against the decay of the flesh from a man whose equally indomitable energy was facing imminent deterioration. It is tempting to imagine Cendrars paraphrasing Flaubert and stating *"Thérèse c'est moi."* But Thérèse's devouring energy and lust is not only manifested in a hypersexuality exacerbated by advancing old age, which would place the creation of her character into the category of self-therapeutic projections. She is, on the contrary, the realization of a fully liberated creativity which she embodies in the unrivalled command of her art and her perpetually renewed inventiveness which transcend all moral or esthetic codes.

II   *The Writer as an Exorcist*

On a deeper and more general level, the gallery of monsters anchored to a spectacular epic of perversity may be interpreted as the product of a final act of creative exorcism through which the exacerbated sensitivity of the writer is liberated from the apocalyptic sense of the destructive forces at work in the modern world. As it has already been noted in the course of this study Cendrars's flaunted admiration for the modern world and the "new regime of personality" he saw emerging in it has always been tempered by his awareness of the "general upheaval of consciousness and intimate disruption of the senses and the heart" inherent to modern man's transformation.[5] The radical dissolution of sensibilities to which the willed relish in depravity and the bravado characterizing that world of freaks bears witness, seems to indicate that Thérèse and her acolytes are scions of Moravagine who had undertaken the task of "ransacking our static houses of time and space . . . forcing the sourish wind of our civilization." (vol. 4, pp. 101, 102) The violence of the portrayal of a world in which "Esthetics are shit sticks" (vol. 14, pp. 224), as the author of the play, Guy de Montauriol, puts it, or in which the debauchery is considered a "divinity, an idol" (p. 80)

apparently warrants the epithet of "Savonarola in Paris" given to
Cendrars by Raymond Dumay in his introduction to the novel (vol.
14, pp. I–V).

A closer reading of the text reveals no vibrations that might
radiate from an ethical indictment on the part of the author; nor is
moral anger aroused in the reader. This has prompted several
reviewers of the book to deplore its lack of metaphysical passion and
see in it "a great deal of schoolboy snook."[6] Without endorsing such
flippant dismissal of the novel's artistic worth, one must certainly
admit that a need for excoriation or exorcism of evil is not the
creative springboard. The parodic artificial existence of the puppet-
like figures makes Cendrars's world irreal. This is a world of
stock-in-trade cardboard stereotypes, pulled out of popular serials,
detective stories, thrillers, exotic tales of adventures, evoking once
more the image of the conjurer's hat. The principle of existence of
the characters bears no relation to an overall *Weltanschaung*. The
raison d'être of this narrative has to be sought elsewhere.

III   *Literary Hedonism*

Taken at face value on the mere level of content *Emmène moi au
bout du monde* could be mistaken for a parodic form of *"littérature
de sensation."* There is, however, artifice and exaggeration inflating
the subject matter which recalls Susan Sontag's definition of Camp
insofar as Camp "incarnates a victory of 'style' over 'content',
'aesthetics' over 'morality', of irony over tragedy."[7] This definition
could apply to any of the major characters in this narrative as well as
to the attitude of the author himself whose creative driving force
appears to spring from an ironical detached stance toward the
function of writing and the sheer delight he takes in irrepressible
word spinning.

In a prefatory note Cendrars states:

This book is written according to the esthetics of someone who believes in
what he is telling, like Coleman Hawkins, saxo-tenor, and his musicians
from heaven. . . . Timeless Jazz. . . . (vol. 14, p. 2)

The reference to jazz is enlightening. Just as a jazz artist surrenders
to his invention in each successive improvisation, the narrator and
his protagonists surrender to an orgastic process of creative storytelling.

To tell a good yarn is a common obsession here; it builds and maintains the picaresque vitality of the text. Thérèse, for instance, gets caught up in exuberant verbal chemistry. These energies are no less unquenchable than her sexual drives. Any audience, responsive or not, serves for her as a pretext to bring out story after story in a constant ejaculation of words: her theories on dramatic art are juxtaposed with the memories of her three former husbands (one of which asked her to emasculate him), of a little girl whose mother (a grocer) used to beat her to tears and shut her up by choking her with a pound of butter, of a one-hundred-three-year-old prince who used to call daily for Thérèse's sexual services to restore his balance in crises of senile delirium. . . . Her visit to the tattoo parlor of the exclergyman-legion deserter, Owen, makes him spark off with extravagant anecdotes about the Legion. Her irruption into Emile's bar leads to the swashbuckling account of his dealings with the police in one of his night brawls. The detective story sketch which fills half of the book after Emile's murder becomes a pretext for more good "rap" while the whole theater company is held for questioning at the police headquarters where Thérèse entertains them all with her torrent of anecdotes.

The novel thus appears like a storytelling carnival. This gives Cendrars's enterprise an essentially ludic character. The playfulness of storytelling for its own sake and the author's impish enjoyment in the writing process could be called, in view of Barthes's theories in the *Pleasure of the Text,* the *"Jouissance"* of the author. What mattered to Cendrars in this last significant work[8] he was to publish was not the erotics of content but the erotics of writing. Instead of producing a violent piece of creative exorcism he indulged in literary hedonism.

CHAPTER 9

Conclusion

A T the end of this panoramic study of Cendrars's works the reader
may be left with the lingering impression that, notwithstanding its vastness and multiplicity, Cendrars's world is a self-enclosed
one. A perusal of the criticism devoted to him throughout the last
fifty years would reinforce that feeling. Even the more recent
studies which give preeminence to the work over the man and
stress Cendrars the writer rather than Cendrars the legend, stay
within the highly individual orbit of the writer's action and creative
activity. Does this confirm the isolation of Cendrars's production in
the twentieth-century world of letters? This view has already been
suggestively expressed by Ferreira de Castro when he states:

At a time when almost every poet inevitably reminds us of others we have
already read, Blaise Cendrars's work appears to us solitary, isolated, like
one of those distant islands of which he likes to speak, an island of a single
owner, where no one before him ever landed.[1]

On the other side of the critics' pendulum one also finds the
opposing tendency to present Cendrars as now the inspirer, now the
forerunner of practically every movement—and at times a con-
tributor to each of them.

Together with the issue of the marginality or the centrality of his
work the question of its modernity is also raised. To some, like
Henry Miller, Cendrars is the "most contemporary of contemporaries."[2] To others, he is "the archetype of an extinct race."[3] In
still others he is:

not behind us as Morand, nor ahead of us. He is rather beside us. . . . His
work resembles his face: it has wrinkles, but these are what are called
"character wrinkles" in the theatre world. Cendrars will not age any
longer.[4]

In a century when literary "isms," schools, and coteries have proliferated, Cendrars indeed deftly escapes all possible classification. Originally steeped in the Symbolist tradition, under the influence of Remy de Gourmont, he broke through the avant-gardes at the beginning of the century without letting any label adhere to him. There are, however, Expressionist tendencies in both his poetic and prose works. The literary creation viewed as the expression of an individual drama, a tortured and morbid imagination which at times recalls the works of Trakl, a greater trust placed in imagination than common sense, the lineage of a Goethe, Nietzsche, Whitman, and Baudelaire are all features common to Cendrars and the Expressionists. The very fact that he was published in *Der Sturm* and *Die Aktion* (the two major Expressionist publications) indicates that they recognized in him a kindred spirit.

Nevertheless, Cendrars never adopted their stylistic experiments, nor did he endorse those of the Dadaists. He has been seen, however, as a forerunner of the Dada spirit and *Moravagine,* as we noted earlier, has been read by some as representing the epitome of the Dada spirit. Since in the words of Tzara himself, "the true Dada were always separated from Dada,"[5] we could invite the reader to view Cendrars, in his proud independence, as the truest embodiment of the Dada spirit. Tzara's profession of faith in the lecture he delivered in Weimar in 1922 could in many respects have also been that of our writer:

Beauty and Truth do not exist; what interests me is the intensity of a personality, directly, clearly transposed into its work, man and his vitality, the angle by which he looks at the elements and the way in which he knows how to pick up sensations and emotions out of the basket of death.[6]

In this light, even Cendrars's later prose works which, at a time when the being of language supersedes man, exhibit a total lack of deference to the received literary ideas of the age, may be viewed as another expression of the Dada spirit.

Yet, Cendrars's scope remains much wider and in a way timeless. There lingers in him a Romantic yearning for the Absolute and a reluctance to deny literature its power of expression and representation of a totality. At the same time, he is also something of an ultramodern word-monger, a manufacturer of texts who heralded the twentieth-century subversion of genres and unabashedly engaged in the art of "re-writing" to such an extent that his work could often illustrate Roland Barthes's statement that: "The writer chooses to make combinations. He combines quotations from which he removes the quotation marks."[7] The supreme paradox of the effect of total originality achieved by Cendrars's "combinations" is in itself indicative of the author's disillusioned clearsightedness about the dynamics of writing in an age of consumerism.

Oscillating between these two extremes of the literary spectrum, his work seems to have come too soon or too late. Hence its apparent isolation. However, its independence from literary formulae in fashion will save it from the risk of obsolescence inherent to all avant-garde movements. When the death of the hero has been accepted as an irreversible fact, he gave life to two of the most archetypal characters in the twentieth-century novel. His own persona, deliberately constructed as the main pillar of his work in days when individual expression is replaced by anonymous voices, stands as both a scornful and playful denunciation of the depersonalizing aspects of the modern world. But it also expresses a lucid and obstinate struggle with the process of writing, an awareness of its limitations and of the mythic character of literary production itself, which characterizes the entire century. As the myth of Cendrars the man disappears, his work will assume an increasingly forceful presence. It is not inappropriate to conclude along with F. J. Temple that "Blaise Cendrars is only starting."[8]

Notes and References

Unless otherwise indicated, quotations from Cendrars's works are my own translations from the *Club Francais du Livre* edition. Volume and page numbers are given in the text.

Chapter One

1. Blaise Cendrars, interview with André Parinaud, "Distinguons les poètes, les aventuriers du dimanche, des explorateurs scientifiques et des mordus du sport," *Arts* (Sept. 12–18, 1952), p. 10.

2. *L'intransigeant* (Dec. 24, 1929), p. 4.

3. Maurice Nadeau and Roland Barthes, "*Où/ou va la littérature?*" in *Dialogues de France Culture, Ecrire . . . Pour quoi? Pour qui?* (Grenoble: Presses Universitaires de Grenoble, 1974), pp. 15, 18.

4. Charles Baudelaire, *Flowers of Evil,* ed. and trans. by M. and J. Matthews (New York: New Directions, 1955), p. 133.

5. John Dos Passos, chapter title in *Orient Express* (New York: Jonathan Cape and Harrison Smith, 1930).

6. Jean Buhler, p. 106.

7. Claude Leroy, "*L'Aventurier de la vie. A travers les romans. De la braise aux cendres,*" *Le Monde* (Feb. 4, 1972), p. 15.

8. See Bochner, Bozon-Scalzitti, Flückiger.

9. Blaise Cendrars, "*Lettres à Sven Stelling Michaud,*" Editeur de *Vol à Voile, Ecriture II* (Vevey, Switzerland: Editions Bertil Galland, 1975), p. 171. Letter dated May 21, 1931.

10. Ibid, p. 175. Letter dated Dec. 14, 1931.

11. Nino Frank, "*Chronique Malles et Valises,*" *Nouvelles Littéraires* (April 21, 1928), p. 5.

12. See Alexandre Eulalio.

13. Bochner, p. 80.

14. "*Enquête,*" *La Révolution Surréaliste,* No. 12 (Dec. 15, 1929), p. 67.

15. Henry Miller, *The Wisdom of the Heart,* p. 152.

16. Conrad Moricand, *Portraits Astrologiques* (Paris: Au Sans Pareil, 1933), p. 35.

Chapter Two

1. *I.S.* p. 211. All further references to this volume in this chapter are given in the text with page numbers only.

2. Jean-Paul Sartre, *Nausea*, trans. Lloyd Alexander (New York: New Directions paper book, 1964), p. 56
3. Published in Moscow in 1909 according to Talvart bibliography and all other Cendrars's bibliographies. The book, however, was never found and may very likely be part of Cendrars's imaginary writings. See Claude Leroy, "Manuel de la bibliographie des livres jamais publiés ni même écrits par Cendrars," *Europe*, No. 566 (June 1976), pp. 153–68.
4. Remy de Gourmont (1858–1915), poet, novelist, dramatist, essayist was closely linked to the Symbolist movement. He was one of the strongest early influences on Cendrars who acknowledged his admiration for him in several of his works.
5. Vol. I, note 17, p. 295.
6. Remy de Gourmont, *Sixtine*, 8th ed. (1890; Paris: Mercure de France, rpt. 1918), p. 47.
7. Cendrars had originally thought of "Alea" or "Allotria" (*I.S.* p. 132). "Alea" figured on the title page of the original manuscript of *Moganni Nameh*. It is impossible to determine when he adopted the final title, borrowed from a 1910 publication, *Moganni Nameh, Novellen und Gedichte*, by Hans Heinz Ewers, a German author of stories steeped in Satanism and Occultism.
8. Yvette Bozon Scalzitti, *Blaise Cendrars et le Symbolisme, de Moganni Nameh au Transsibérien.*
9. André Malraux, *Les Voix du Silence* (Paris: N.R.F., 1951), pp. 309–10.

Chapter Three

1. "*Panama et l'aventure de mes sept oncles,*" Vol. 1, 51.
2. "*1913, pourquoi écrire, poète?*" in *L'Année 1913 Les formes esthétiques de l'oeuvre d'art à la veille de la première guerre mondiale,* Liliane Brion Guerry ed. (Paris: Klincksieck, 1977), Vol. I., 586.
3. All quotations from this poem are taken from Walter Albert, *Selected Writings,* trans. Scott Bates, pp. 47–65.
4. Started by Jules Romains's declaration, in a lecture he gave in Brussels in 1923, that Cendrars determined Apollinaire's "change of front" in "Zone," the debate over the question of respective influences between the two poets has engaged over fifteen scholars. On Cendrars's side: Robert Goffin, Jacques Henry Levesque, Jean Louis Parrot, James Lawler, Pär Bergman, Robert Couffignal, Max Pol Fouchet. On Apollinaire's side: André Billy, Marcel Adéma, Pascal Pia, Scott Bates, Margaret Davies. Michel Decaudin, Marc Poupon, and Marie Jeanne Durry remained neutral.

Apollinaire was correcting the proofs of "Zone" in November 1912 when Cendrars's poem came out at his "*Edition des Hommes Nouveaux.*" The two poets knew each other by that time, but it has been impossible to determine the exact date of their first meeting. The dates of composition cannot be conclusively determined for lack of documents, available at the present time to scholars, which would confirm or infirm the date set down by the author. The publication of *Inédits Secrets* would rather confirm the reader's doubt. No mention of the poem is made in the volume and the play *Danse Macabre de l'amour* bears the same dates of composition, April 6–8, 1912, as the manuscript of *Les Pâques* at the Fonds Doucet, Bibliothèque Sainte-Geneviève. It is difficult to believe that such an immature drama and a poem of the calibre attained by Cendrars in this work would have been simultaneously conceived.

A study of internal evidence has not been conclusive either. Scott Bates's contention (*Apollinaire*, TWAS; New York: Twayne, 1967, note 4, pp. 181–82) that it favors Apollinaire is contradicted by the fundamental divergences in the two poets' attitudes toward modernity at that time. The detailed comparative analysis of the two poems, made by Marie Jeanne Durry, confirms our position. The similarities she noted are greatly outweighed by the thematic and stylistic differences. See Marie Jeanne Durry, *Guillaume Apollinaire, Alcools* (Paris: SEDES, 1956), Vol. 1, pp. 234–301.

What precludes most decisively the theory of an influence of "Zone" on Cendrars's poem is the striking similitude between some pages of *Moganni Nameh* and *Pâques à New York* which has been pointed out by Yvette Bozon Scalzitti. The theme of the writer's identification with Christ's passion, the walk through a city, the appeal in vain to the Virgin Mary, the loneliness and fear of the writer are all present in the third chapter of the novel, which can be read as a rough draft of the poem. This earlier reference to Easter Sunday may account for the more general title, *Les Pâques*. It could be argued that since *Moganni Nameh* was only published chapter by chapter in the French review *Les Feuilles Libres* in 1922, nothing proves that the final version of the novel was completed in 1911–1912 as suggested in *Inédits Secrets*. Here, however, internal evidence is irrefutable: the blatant immaturity of style leaves no doubt as to the earlier date of the prose composition.

The state of spiritual disquietude that underlines Cendrars's poem was not a literary stance either. An entry in the New York diaries on March 5, 1912 confirms its prior existence. Quoting Descartes's cosmological argument in favor of the existence of God (the fact that I exist proves that God exists) in the thirty-sixth section of the third *Méditation Métaphysique*, Cendrars ends it with two exclamation marks, a question mark, and the following comment:

This at the most demonstrates the duality of my nature and my desire, my feeling, my ideas of unity: i.e. the nostalgic need to fill in my inner form, to calm my malaise. . . ."

(*I.S.* p. 203)

The final notes on this page throw an equally revealing light on the trajectory of the future poet's thought during the months that preceded the creation of *Pâques à New York*. After a comment on Gérard de Nerval, he lists himself ("me"), after O. Uzanne (probably a misreading of Cendrars's writing of Uz Johann, an Anacreontic German poet of the eighteenth century), Hans Heinz Ewers from whom he borrowed the title of *Moganni Nameh* (see note 7, chapter two) and Claudel.

5. Charles Henri Hirsch, rev. of the poem, *Mercure de France*, September 1, 1919, No. 135, p. 139.

6. *Poème et drame* (Paris: Eugène Figuière et Cie, May 1913), Vol. 4.

7. *Gil Blas*, July 1, 1914. The "polemic of Simultaneism," which lasted from April 1913 to July 1914, reached its peak between October and December 1913 after the publication of the poem in September. Some twenty-five letters and lampoons from André Billy, André Salmon, Pierre Lévy, Paul Fort, Beaudoin, Hertz, Guilbeaux, Fernand Divoire, and an anonymous group, the Antagonists, which undoubtedly included Henri Martin Barzun, filled the columns of *Paris Journal, Paris Midi, Gil Blas, La Liberté*. Cendrars and Sonia Delaunay answered André Salmon in *Gil Blas* in October; in November, *Der Sturm* published an article of Cendrars in which he denounced the "grubbers and arrivists." Cendrars had also prepared a chronology and an article on the simultaneous contrasts for *Les Soirées de Paris*, but Apollinaire finally did not publish it. The Futurists joined the debate in December with an article, "*Simultanéité futuriste*," published in *Der Sturm*. In June 1914, the publication of "*Simultanéisme-librettisme*" by Apollinaire in *Les Soirées de Paris* revived the quarrel which became then mainly an argument between Barzun and Apollinaire in *Paris Journal* and *Le Temps*. It was finally brought to a close by the rumbles of the war. In addition to the volumes of Pär Bergman and Léon Somville which provide a detailed analysis of the subject, consult Sidoti Antonio, "*La Prose du Transsibérien de Blaise Cendrars*," *Lettres Romanes*, 27, No. 1 (February 1973), 71–84; Monique Chefdor, "*Blaise Cendrars et le Simultaneisme*," *Europe*, No. 566, pp. 24–29; *Inédits Secrets*, pp. 353–75.

8. *Poème et Drame*, p. 16.

9. "The Homer of the Transsiberian," *Orient Express* (New York: Jonathan Cape and Hamon Smith, 1930), p. 161.

10. Walter Albert, *Selected Writings*, Intro. pp. 15–19.

11. All quotations from this poem are taken from the translation of Walter Albert in *Selected Writings*, pp. 67–99.

12. Jean Cocteau, *Carte Blanche* (Lausanne: Mermod, 1953), p. 146.

13. Fernand Divoire, *Le Grenier de Montjoie!* (Paris: Edition du carnet critique, 1919), p. 12.

14. All quotations from *Panama* are taken from Walter Albert, *Selected Writings*, trans. John Dos Passos, pp. 101–37.

15. Vol. 14, pp. 305–17. The author's wife, Raymone, asserts that she has seen letters from these uncles.

16. Albert T' Serstevens, p. 42.

17. *Futurist Manifestoes,* ed. Umbro Apollonio (New York: Viking Press, 1973), p. 100.

18. Quotations from the *Poèmes Elastiques* are taken from Walter Albert, *Selected Writings,* pp. 139–83.

19. Fernand Léger, *Functions of Painting,* trans. Alexandra Anderson (New York: Viking Press, 1973), p. 35.

20. Jean Pierre Goldenstein, "*De l'élasticité poétique. Genèse d'un poéme de Blaise Cendrars,*" *Lettres Romanes,* 24, No. 1 (Feb. 1970), 73–79; "*Blaise Cendrars sur les traces du Capitaine Cook,*" *Revue d'histoire littéraire de la France,* January–February 1973, pp. 112–17; "*Vers une systématique du poème élastique,*" *Europe,* No. 566, pp. 115–30.

21. Henri Béhar, "*Débris, collage et invention poétique,*" *Europe* No. 566, pp. 102–14.

22. Paul Fierens, *NRF* (August 1924), p. 223.

23. A first mention of Francis Lacassin's discovery appeared in Hubert Juin, "*Trois cent volumes et des poussières,*" *Les Lettres Françaises,* No. 1141 (21–27 July, 1966), pp. 12–13. Since, however, two articles by Francis Lacassin discuss the matter at length and give details about the relationship of Cendrars and Le Rouge: "*Quand la poésie copie le feuilleton,*" *Le magazine littéraire* No. 9 (July August 1967), p. 23 and "*Gustave Le Rouge: le gourou secret de Blaise Cendrars,*" *Europe,* No. 566, pp. 71–93. In the same issue of *Europe,* pp. 94–101, Francis Lacassin gave a fragment of a still unpublished critical edition of "*Documentaires*" in which he juxtaposed the two texts, entitled *Les poèmes du Docteur Cornélius par Blaise Cendrars et Gustave Le Rouge.*

24. T'Serstevens, *L'homme que fut Blaise Cendrars* (Paris Denoël, 1972), p. 42. Yvette Bozon Scalzitti, *Blaise Cendrars ou la Passion de l'écriture* (Lausanne: L'Age d'homme, 1977), Appendice C, pp. 297–309.

25. Gustave Le Rouge, *Le mystérieux Docteur Cornélius* (Paris: 10/18, Union Générale d'Editions, 1975), Vol. 1, 49–50.

26. *Complete Postcards,* p. 63.

27. See note 21.

28. Paul Morand, Intro. to *Du Monde Entier, Poésies complètes, 1912–1924* (Paris: Gallimard, 1968), p. II.

29. See "Bibliographical note on Ocean Letters," *Complete Postcards,* p. 251. All following quotations from *Feuilles de Route* refer to this publication, pp. 118–241.

30. A contradictory point of view has been advanced by the Brazilian scholar Alexandre Eulalio who found several thematic and stylistic affinities between *Feuilles de Route* and some of Oswald de Andrade's poems in *Pau Brasil,* published in 1925 in Paris by Cendrars's publisher "Au Sans Pareil." See *L'aventure brésilienne de Blaise Cendrars* (Rennes, Etudes portugaises et brésiliennes, V. Faculté des lettres et Sciences Humaines, Université de Rennes, 1969), note 26, p. 32.

Relationships between Cendrars and the Brazilian Modernists have also been discussed by Aracy A. Amaral in her book *Blaise Cendrars no Brasil e os Modernistas*. The more recent volume published by Alexandre Eulalio, *A Aventura Brasileira de Blaise Cendrars*, brings out more parallels between Oswald de Andrade and Blaise Cendrars (pp. 58–59). Reprints in the same volume of articles published in the Brazilian press during Cendrars's visits there also confirm Cendrars's strong impact on his Brazilian contemporaries.

According to the testimony of Cendrars's friends (Sergio Buarque de Hollanda, Rubens Borba de Moraes, Yan Almeida de Prado, Luis da Silva Prado), interviewed during our visit to Brazil in May 1975, Cendrars's enthusiasm for Brazil was overwhelming. He imposed his own vision of the country on his hosts and encouraged them to write about their own land instead of imitating the Parisian moderns. We feel, therefore, that, in this case, the parallels between the Brazilian and the French poet may not be a matter of textual inspiration, but rather a coincidental result of their friendship and their travels together.

Chapter Four

1. James Harding, *The Ox on the Roof* (London: Macdonald, 1972), p. 57.

2. Philippe Soupault, *"Enfin, Cendrars vint . . . ou tel qu'en lui-même enfin,"* *Mercure de France*, No. 1185 (May 1962), pp. 85–87.

3. Pierre Reverdy, *Nord-Sud* No. 9 (November 1917); (rpt. Paris: Flammarion, 1975), p. 64.

4. Quoted by Henri Béhar, *"Sur un inédit patent,"* *Europe* No. 566, p. 189. The letters to Jacques Doucet and the original manuscript are in the Fonds Doucet, bibliothèque Sainte Geneviève.

5. According to Jacqueline Chadourne, Cyrano de Bergerac's *L'autre monde, Etats et Empires de la lune, Etats et Empires du Soleil* was mentioned in Cendrars's reading notes as early as 1907. Since the 1650 utopian novel was published in its complete form only in 1921, Cendrars would have sought access to one of the rare editions of 1657 or 1662, a fact that confirms the seriousness of his attraction to such literature.

6. The appendix, divided in three parts: *"Histoire du Perpetuum Mobile," "Définition du Perpetuum Mobile"* and *"Origine de l'idée de Perpetuum Mobile"* remained unpublished at the Jacques Doucet library until the last two parts were presented by Henry Béhar in *Europe*, No. 566, pp. 204–08.

7. See Richard Abel, "American Film and the French Literary Avant Garde," *Contemporary Literature* No. 1, Vol. 17, (Winter 1976), 84–109; Pierre Quesnoy, *Littérature et Cinéma* (Paris: Editions Le Rouge et le Noir, 1928) and Jean Epstein, *Ecrits sur le cinéma, 1921–1953* (Paris: Seghers, Cinéma Club, 1974), Vol. 1.

8. A plan of the projected script has been published in *I.S.* pp. 410–12.

9. Abel Gance, *"Blaise Cendrars et le cinéma,"* *Mercure de France*, No. 1185, pp. 170–71.

10. Fernand Léger, *"Réponse à une enquête de René Clair,"* *Europe*, No. 508–09 (August September 1971).

11. While in Rome Cendrars was also instrumental in securing contracts for the actor Marcel Levesque in other productions, which confirms his association with the Rinascimento studios, sometimes questioned because of the nonexistence of *La Vénus Noire*.

12. *"Le mystère de l'Ange Notre-Dame,"* *La Caravane*, October 1916. A second part appeared in December 1918: *"Le film de la fin du monde,"* *Mercure de France*, Vol. 130, 419–30.

13. Francis Vanoye, *"Le cinéma de Cendrars,"* *Europe*, No. 566, p. 188.

14. See *Moravagine*, Vol. 4, p. 265; *Dan Yack*, Vol. 5, 248–70; *Trop c'est trop*, Vol. 14, 67–71. During our May 1975 stay in Brazil, all surviving friends of Cendrars interviewed affirmed that he did not even speak of such a project during his visits there and made no effort to contact officials to launch it.

15. André Parinaud, *"La peinture et ses témoins,"* *Arts*, No. 333 (November 16, 1951).

16. Martin Steins, *Blaise Cendrars, bilans nègres* (Paris: Archives des Lettres Modernes, No. 169, Minard), p. 13.

17. Ibid., p. 5.

18. Martin Steins's study aptly demonstrates that Cendrars's compilation is not as accurately scientific as the detailed bibliography presented by the author would have the reader believe. See Steins, p. 14.

19. Ibid., p. 21.

20. See Bernard Mouralis, *"Notes sur l'Anthologie Nègre,"* *Europe*, No. 566, pp. 169–78.

21. An unpublished copy of it is in the Fonds Jacques Doucet.

22. James Harding, *The Ox on the Roof* (London: MacDonald, 1972), p. 59.

Chapter Five

1. André Breton, *Manifestoes of Surrealism*, trans. Richard Seaver and Helen Lane (Ann Arbor: University of Michigan Press, 1969), p. 6.

2. Hugues Richard, *"Cendrars et le fabuleux Général Sutter,"* *Europe*, No. 566, pp. 35–49. As Hugues Richard's juxtaposition of some passages shows, several pages are nothing but a literal translation of Birmann's text from which, Richard notes, Cendrars also borrowed the misspelling of Sutter's name with one "t."

3. James Peter Zollinger, *Sutter, the Man and his Empire* (Oxford: Oxford University Press, 1939).

4. Ibid., note 1, p. 5.

5. Remy de Gourmont's influence has been pointed out several times by Yvette Bozon-Scalzitti and Jean Carlo Flückiger. The adaptation of Ivan Bloch's book was discussed by Steve Bellstrom in "Moravagine, Mascha and *The Sexual Life of our Time,*" Blaise Cendrars special session seminar, MLA Convention, New York, Dec. 29, 1976.

6. See Henri Béhar, "*Sur un inédit patent*" and "*Un appendice inédit de Blaise Cendrars,*" *Europe,* No. 566, pp. 197–208.

7. Jay Bochner, pp. 41, 156–57.

8. Jean Louis Parrot, *Blaise Cendrars,* p. 50.

9. See Jean Carlo Flückiger.

10. Claude Leroy, "*Figures de Dan Yack, Le jeu dans l'ile,*" in *Cendrars aujourd'hui, présence d'un romancier,* ed. Michel Decaudin (Paris: Lettres Modernes, Minard, 1977), pp. 109–44.

11. Raoul Celly, rev. of *Le Plan de l'Aiguille, La Revue Nouvelle,* No. 53–54 (Dec. 1929–Jan. 1930).

12. Bochner, p. 172.

13. Bochner, p. 181. Originally in *Diogène* (April 19, 1946), p. 5. Also quoted by Jean Buhler, Jean Louis Parrot, and Claude Leroy (see note 10).

14. Victor Ehrlich, *Russian Formalism, History, Doctrine* (The Hague, 1965), pp. 240–41.

15. Jean Louis Parrot, p. 55.

16. Victor Segalen, *La grande statuaire chinoise,* n.p. Quoted by Henry Bouillier, Intro. to *Stèles* (Paris: Plon, 1963), p. 17.

17. Blaise Cendrars, Preface to *Poto Poto* by Eric Von Stroheim (Paris: La Fontaine, 1956), p. 9.

18. Henry Lefebvre, *Vers le Cybernanthrope* (Paris: Denoel-Gonthier, 1967, 1971), pp. 197–98.

19. Henry Miller, *The Wisdom of the Heart,* pp. 157, 152.

Chapter Six

1. Cendrars published two volumes in the collection *Les Têtes Brûlées: Feu le Lieutenant Bringolf,* 1930, adapted and trans. by Cendrars and *Al Capone, le balafré,* 1931, adapted by Cendrars and introduced by Geo London. Two more translations adapted by Cendrars were published by Grasset: *Hors la loi,* 1936, Al Jennings's *Through the Shadows with O'Henry* and *Forêt Vierge,* 1938, Ferreira de Castro's *A Selva.*

2. "Carolina," *La Revue Nouvelle,* No. 66 (March 1931), pp. 8–13. "1914," *Nouvel Age,* No. 11 (November 1931), pp. 1026–29. "Cassandre," *Orbes,* No. 3 (2nd series, 1933).

3. *Playboy,* Interview with Truman Capote, Vol. 15, No. 3 (March 1968), 56.

4. See André Fontaine, *The Art of Non Fiction* (New York: Thomas Crowell, 1974), pp. 4–5.

5. First published in *Navire d'Argent*, No. 11 (April 1926), pp. 285–98. Incorporated the same year in the chapter "*Randonnées d'Amérique*" in *Moravagine* and reprinted in the collection of essays *Aujourd'hui* (1931).
6. *La Petite Gironde, Le Petit Marseillais, Le Républicain Orléanais, La Dépêche algérienne, La Vigie Marocaine, Le Mémorial de Saint Etienne, La Dépêche de Brest.*

Chapter Seven

1. Nino Frank, "*Une mort difficile,*" *Mémoire Brisée* (Paris: Calman Lévy, 1967), p. 217.
2. Guillaume Apollinaire, "*L'adieu du cavalier,*" *Calligrames, Poèmes* (Paris: Livre de poche, 1956), p. 146.
3. Photographs of Febronio from the *Archivos do Manicomio Judiciario do Rio de Janeiro* can be seen in *Um Livro 100% Brasileiro*, trans. and ed. by Teresa Thieriot with commentaries by Alexandre Eulalio (Sao Paulo: Editora Perspectiva, 1976) pp. 169, 170 and in *A Aventura Brasileira de Blaise Cendrars*, Alexandre Eulalio, p. 30. In the same volume, Alexandre Eulalio confirms the facts about Febronio's internment in Rio de Janeiro's penitentiary and his authorship of *Revelacoes do Principe do Fogo*, a book immediately withdrawn from the market by the State censorship but considered by young intellectuals of the time, such as Sergio Buarque de Hollanda and Prudente de Morais, as "a native example of the best Surrealism" (p. 31). Alexandre Eulalio even avers that Cendrars's story of Febronio may be considered a "quasi reportage" (p. 31). Although no official document on Cendrars's interview with Febronio at the penitentiary has come to light, the fact that one occurred was confirmed by Sergio Buarque de Hollanda when the author interviewed him in Sao Paulo on May 22, 1975.
4. From a different angle, a recent study of Cendrars's Brazilian vocabulary points out the "manichean vision of things" in his Brazilian texts. See Mariza Veiga, *Le lexique brésilien de Blaise Cendrars*, Intro. by Jean Richer (Nice: Centre du XXe siécle, 1977), p. 5.
5. Rubens Borba de Moraes, "*Recodacoes de Blaise Cendrars,*" in *José, Litteratura Critica e Arte* (Rio de Janeiro: No. 9, December 1977), p. 46. According to all testimony gathered in Brazil during the author's visit in 1975, Cendrars's travels in Brazil were limited to the areas surrounding Sao Paulo and Rio de Janeiro and the ports of call along the coast from Belem to Santos. The only island trip he made was the journey to Minais Gerais with a group of Modernist artists and writers during Easter week in 1924.
6. In *A Aventura Brasileira de Blaise Cendrars*, Alexandre Eulalio discloses several sources of Cendrars's Brazilian stories. *Coronel* Bento, for instance, is Bento Canavarro, a manager of *Conseilheiro* Prado's fazendas (p. 32). The living model for Oswaldo Padroso could have been Luis Bueno

de Miranda who bought the *fazenda* Morro Azul from the Prado Chaves Cy
(p. 52). A poem by Oswald de Andrade which contains all the thematic
elements of *"La Tour Eiffel sidérale"* is also quoted (p. 50).

7. Elizabeth Hardwick, "Sad Brazil," *New York Review of Books* (June
27, 1974), p. 10.

8. See note 30, chapter three.

9. See chapter three p. 54.

10. In *Vol à Voile*, Cendrars had amplified the legend started with the
poem. He again picks up the legendary episodes of the train rides with
Rogovine, but hints for the first time that he had a job in Saint Petersburg.
The street name is correct and Leouba obviously stands for Leuba, the
jeweller for whom he worked.

11. The story announced here as that of Maripuru will become "Caru-
muru" published first in *La Table Ronde* No. 47 (November 1951), and
incorporated in *Le Brésil* (Monaco: Les documents d'arts, 1952).

12. See Micheline Tison Braun, *Tristan Tzara, inventeur de l'Homme
Nouveau* (Paris: Nizet, 1977).

13. The Bollandists' *"Acta Sanctorum"* published in Belgium since 1653
and Olivier Leroy, *La lévitation* (Juvisy: Editions du Cerf, 1928).

14. Jay Bochner, p. 216.

15. Jean Carlo Fluckiger, p. 165.

Chapter Eight

1. *Trop c'est trop*, published in 1957 after the writer's first paralytic
attack, does not bring out any new element in Cendrars's writings. It is
mostly a collection of articles published from time to time by Cendrars in
various literary reviews or travel magazines.

2. *Nouvelles Littéraires* (February 21, 1956).

3. Yvette Bozon Scalzitti recently disclosed how much Cendrars had
borrowed from Robert Kemp's introduction to the actress' book *Souvenirs
de ma vie*. See *Blaise Cendrars ou la Passion de l'écriture*, note 301, p. 352.

4. Ibid., p. 274.

5. The statement, first made in 1929 in a note on the French Novel,
Vol. 6, p. 35, reappears verbatim in the twelfth chapter of the novel, Vol.
14, p. 233.

6. Hilary Corke, rev. of *Emmène-moi au bout du monde*, *The Listener*
(March 2, 1967), p. 301.

7. Susan Sontag, *Against Interpretation* (New York, Noonday Press,
Farrar, Strauss and Giroux, 1961), p. 287.

8. While writing *Emmène-moi au bout du monde*, Cendrars's interest
turned to the dramatic form. He collaborated with Nino Frank on three
plays for the radio: *Sarajevo* (January 1955), *Gilles de Rais* (December 1955)
and *Le Divin Arétin* (June 1957). Violence, eroticism, general rebellion
against standard norms evoked by the subject matter of these plays fall in

line with Cendrars's favorite themes. It is difficult, however, to assess the exact degree of Cendrars's contribution to the writing of these plays.

Chapter Nine

1. Ferreira de Castro, *"Hommage à Blaise Cendrars,"* *Risques,* (26, May 1954), p. 18.

2. Henry Miller, "Tribute to Blaise Cendrars," *The Wisdom of the Heart* (New York: New Directions, 1941), p. 152.

3. Robert Marteau, *"Vie et mort de Blaise Cendrars,"* *Esprit,* No. 29 (March 1961), p. 456.

4. Max Pol Fouchet, *"Cendrars, un brahmane à rebours,"* *L'Express,* No. 502 (January 26, 1961), p. 28.

5. Tristan Tzara, lecture delivered in Weimar, September 23, 1932. Repr., *Lampisteries* (Pauvert, 1963), p. 136.

6. Ibid., p. 140.

7. Roland Barthes, *"Où /ou va la littérature?"*, *Ecrire. . ., pour quoi? pour qui?* (Grenoble: Presses Universitaries de Grenoble, 1974), p. 19.

8. F. J. Temple, *"Blaise Cendrars commence,"* *Mercure de France,* No. 1185 (May 1962), p. 192.

Selected Bibliography

PRIMARY SOURCES

Only first editions and recent reprints in paperback are listed here. For a complete bibliography consult Vol. XV of the *Complete Works*, Club Français du Livre and "*Chronologie et bibliographie*," *Europe*, No. 566, pp. 223–48. Unless otherwise indicated, the place of publication is Paris.

1. Cendrars's works in French

1912   *Les Pâques*, Editions des Hommes Nouveaux.
1913   *La Prose du Transsibérien et de la Petite Jehanne de France*, Editions des Hommes Nouveaux.
            Séquences, Editions des Hommes nouveaux.
1916   *La guerre au Luxembourg*, Niestlé.
1917   *Profond Aujourd'hui*, A la belle édition.
1918   *Le Panama ou les aventures de mes sept oncles*, Editions de la Sirène.
            J'ai tué, A la belle édition.
1919   *De Monde Entier ("Les Pâques à New York," Prose du Transsibérien, "Panama"*), Editions de la Nouvelle Revue Francaise.
            Dix neuf poèmes élastiques, Au Sans Pareil.
            La fin du monde filmée par l'ange Notre-Dame, Editions de la Sirène.
1921   *L'anthologie nègre*, Editions de la Sirène (Livre de Poche, 1972).
1921–22 *La perle fiévreuse*, Signaux de France et de Belgique (Nos. 7, 9, 10, 11–12).
1922   *Moganni Nameh*, Les Feuilles Libres (Nos. 26, 27, 28, 29, 30).
1924   *Kodak (Documentaires)*, Stock, Dellamain, Boutelleau.
            Le Formose (Part I of Feuilles de Route), Au Sans Pareil.
1925   *L'Or*, Grasset (Livre de Poche, 1958).
1926   *Moravagine*, Grasset (Livre de Poche, 1957).
            L'A B C du cinéma, Les Ecrivains Réunis.
            L'Eubage, Au Sans Pareil.
            Eloge de la vie dangereuse, Les Ecrivains Réunis.
            "Sao Paulo" (Part II of *Feuilles de Route*), catalogue of Tarsila exhibit, Galerie Percier.
1927–28 *Feuilles de Route* (last section), *Montparnasse* (Nos. 49 & 51).

1928   *Petits contes nègres pour les enfants des Blancs*, Editions du
        Portique.
1929   *Le Plan de l'Aiguille*, Au Sans Pareil.
        Les confessions de Dan Yack, Au Sans Pareil.
        Une nuit dans la forêt, Editions du Verseau (Livre de poche,
        1975).
1930   *Rhum*, Grasset (Livre de Poche, 1963).
        Comment les Blancs sont d'anciens Noirs, Au Sans Pareil.
1931   *Aujourd'hui*, Grasset.
        La création du monde, in Ballets Suédois, Editions du Trianon.
1932   *Vol à voiles*, Lausanne, Payot (Livre de poche, 1975: *Vol à voile*).
1935   *Panorama de la pègre*, Arthaud.
1936   *Hollywood, la Mecque du cinéma*, Grasset.
1937   *Histoires vraies*, Grasset.
1938   *La vie dangereuse*, Grasset.
1940   *D'oultremer à indigo*, Grasset.
        Chez l'armée anglaise, Correa.
1944   *Poésies complètes de Blaise Cendrars*, Intro. by Jacques Henry
        Levesque, Denoël.
1945   *L'Homme foudroyé*, Denoel (Livre de poche, 1960).
1946   *La Main coupée*, Denoel (Folio Gallimard, 1975).
1948   *Bourlinguer*, Denoël (Livre de poche, 1969).
1949   *Le lotissement du ciel*, Denoël (Folio Gallimard, 1976).
        La banlieue de Paris, Lausanne, Guilde du livre and Seghers
        (Introduction to 130 photographs by Robert Doisneau).
1952   *Blaise Cendrars vous parle*, Denoël (Interviews with Michel
        Manoll).
        Le Brésil, Monaco, Les documents d'art (Introduction to 105
        photographs by Jean Manzon).
1953   *Noël aux quatre coins du monde*, Robert Cayla.
1956   *Emmène-moi au bout du monde*, Denoël (Folio, Gallimard, 1974).
        *Entretiens de Fernand Léger avec Blaise Cendrars et Louis Carré
        sur le paysage dans l'oeuvre de Léger*, Louis Carré.
1957   *Trop c'est trop*, Denoël.
        De monde entier au coeur du monde (Complete poems), Denoël.
        Paperback edition: *Du Monde entier, Au coeur du monde*, Poésie
        Gallimard, 1967, 1968.
1958   *A l'aventure* (selections from prose works), Denoël and Club des
        Jeunes Amis du Livre.
1959   *Films sans images*, Denoël.
1960–65 *Oeuvres Complètes*, 8 vols. Denoël.
1968–71 *Oeuvres Completes*, 15 vols., Club Français du Livre with Intro.
        by Raymond Dumay, numerous testimonies from friends and
        writers, abundant iconography.
1969   *Inédits Secrets*, ed. Miriam Cendrars, Club Français du Livre.

2. English Translations

1919   *I have Killed (J'ai tué).* Trans. Harold Ward, *The Plowshare*, No.
        6/7.
1922   *Profound Today (Profond Aujourd'hui).* Trans. Harold Loeb,
        Broom I, No. 3 (January), pp. 265–67.
        "The Cabinet of Doctor Caligari." Rev. of the film, trans. from *Les
        Feuilles Libres*, 4, No. 26 (June–July 1922), *Broom* II, No. 24
        (July), p. 351.
        At the Antipodes of Unity (L'Eubage). Trans. Matthew Josephson,
        Broom, III, No. 3 (October), pp. 182–93.
1926   "The Days of 49" (abridged version of *L'Or*), Hearst's *Interna-
        tional* combined with *Cosmopolitan* (October). *Sutter's Gold
        (L'Or).* Trans. Henry Longan Stuart. New York: Harper, rpr.,
        1936, 1954; London, Heinemann, rpr. New York, Grosset &
        Dunlap, 1936.
1927   *African Saga (Anthologie nègre).* Trans. Margery Bianco. New
        York: Boards Payson & Clark. Rpr. New York: Negro University
        Press, 1969).
1929   *Little Black Stories for Little White Children (Petits contes nègres
        pour les enfants des Blancs).* New York: Harcourt Brace.
1931   *Panama ("La Prose du Transsibérien," "Panama," excerpts from
        Kodak* and from Part I of *Feuilles de Route).* Trans., intro. and
        illust., John Dos Passos. New York: Harper. Rpr. with intro. by
        George Reavey, *Chelsea Review*, No. 3 (Winter 1959), pp. 3–25.
        "John Paul Jones," *European Caravan.* Ed. Samuel Putnam. New
        York: Brewer, Warren & Putnam, pp. 199–204.
        I Have no Regrets (Feu le lieutenant Bringolf). Trans. Warre B.
        Wells, ed. Blaise Cendrars. London: Jarrolds.
1948   *Antarctic Fugue (Le Plan de l'Aiguille).* Trans. unsigned. London:
        Pushkin Press; New York: Anglobooks.
1962   *Selected Writings ("Pâques à New York," "La prose du Transsibé-
        rien,"* two poems from *Documentaires*, five from *Feuilles de route*,
        selections from prose works). Ed. and intro., Walter Albert.
        Preface by Henry Miller. New York: New Directions. Rpr., 1966.
1966   *To the End of the World (Emmène-moi au bout du monde).* Trans.
        Alan Brown. London: Peter Owen; New York: Grove Press, 1968.
        "The Art of Fiction" and "Manolo Secca" (selections from *Blaise
        Cendrars vous parle* and *L'Homme foudroyé* respectively), eleven
        poems. Trans. Ron Padgett, intro. William Brandon. *Paris Review*
        X, No. 37, 105–143.
1968   *Moravagine.* Trans. Alan Brown. London: Peter Owen; New
        York: Doubleday, 1970; London: Penguin Modern Classics Series,
        1979.
        "Two Portraits: Gustave Le Rouge and Arthur Cravan" (from

L'Homme foudroyé and *Le lotissement du ciel*). Trans. William Brandon, *Paris Review* XI, No. 42, 157–70.

"Four poems." Trans. Tom Clark and Ron Padgett, *Works*, I, No. 3, 39–42.

"The Transsiberian Express." Trans. Anselm Holls, *Evergreen Review Reader*. New York: Grove Press, pp. 621–630.

1970   *The Astonished Man (L'homme foudroyé)*. Trans. Nina Rootes. London: Peter Owen.

1972   *Planus (Bourlinguer)*. Trans. Nina Rootes. London: Peter Owen.

"The Prose of the Transsiberian and of Little Jehanne de France." Poem and article with the same title from *Der Sturm*, No. 184–85 (November 1913). Trans. Roger Kaplan, *Chicago Review*, 24, No. 3, 3–21.

1973   *Lice (La Main coupée)*. Trans. Nina Rootes. London: Peter Owen.

1976   *Complete Postcards from the Americas. Poems of Road and Sea (Documentaires, Feuilles de Route, "Sud-Americaines")*. Trans. and intro., Monique Chefdor. Berkeley, Los Angeles, London: University of California Press.

1979   *Selected Poems*. Trans. Peter Hoida, intro. Mary Ann Caws. London: Penguin.

SECONDARY SOURCES

1. Critical works

AMARAL, ARACY. *Blaise Cendrars no Brasil e os modernistas*. Sao Paulo: Martins, 1970. Informative account of Cendrars's visits to Brazil and his relationship with the Modernists.

BOCHNER, JAY. *Blaise Cendrars, Discovery and Re-Creation*. Toronto, Buffalo, London: University of Toronto Press, 1978. The first full-length study of Cendrars in English. Although fact is willfully not distinguished from fiction in the biographical section, the documentation is rich and the personality of the author is perceptively projected. The analysis of *Dan Yack* in relation to Jung's idea of the Modern Man and the application of Buber's distinction between the I/thou and the I/it to Cendrars's later prose writings is particularly interesting.

BOZON-SCALZITTI, YVETTE. *Blaise Cendrars et le Symbolisme*. Paris: Archives des Lettres Modernes, No. 137, Minard, 1972. A professional analysis of the sources of Blaise Cendrars's inspiration in *Moganni Nameh, Séquences* and *Les Pâques*. Thematic affinities between *Moganni Nameh, Les Pâques*, and *Prose du Transsibérien* are indicated for the first time.

——— *Blaise Cendrars ou la Passion de l'Ecriture*. Lausanne: L'Age d'homme, 1977. The most thorough deciphering of Cendrars's prose works to date. The interplay of the self and the other (the man who writes) is subtly projected. The study, however, with its persistent cross references and reliance on thematic interweavings, is accessible only to the specialists of Cendrars.

BUHLER, JEAN. *Blaise Cendrars, homme libre, poète au coeur du monde.* Bienne, Switzerland: Edition du Panorama, 1960. Although incomplete, the first biography which attempts to be accurate. Literary comments remain general and overly eulogistic.

CHADOURNE, JACQUELINE. *Blaise Cendrars, poète du Cosmos.* Paris: Seghers, 1973. The forces of dream and imagination in the life and works of Cendrars. Smooth, easy reading. Informative but the critical analysis is too frequently reduced to paraphrasing or quoting of the text.

EULALIO, ALEXANDRE. *A Aventura Brasileira de Blaise Cendrars.* Sao Paulo, Brasilia: Edicoes Quiron and Instituto Nacional do Livro, 1978. Essential volume on Cendrars and Brazil. Parallels between Oswald de Andrade and Cendrars's poems are discussed. The chronology of Cendrars's activities in Brazil and reprints of articles from the Brazilian press are precious documents.

FLUCKIGER, JEAN CARLO. *Au coeur du texte. Essai sur Blaise Cendrars.* Neuchatel: A la Baconnière, 1977. One of the most illuminating probings into the dynamics of the Cendrarian text. Mostly centered on an analysis of *Moravagine,* the study shows how Cendrars's works are essentially an attempt to conquer the world through the written word and a questioning of the function of writing which endlessly spirals around a central void.

LEVESQUE, JACQUES HENRY. *Blaise Cendrars, Etude suivie d'une anthologie des plus belles pages.* Editions de la Nouvelle Revue Critique, 1947. Along with the introduction to *Du Monde entier au coeur du monde* (see primary sources), the first significant presentation of Cendrars the man and the writer. Although often prone to hyperbolic praise, this volume remains an enlightening landmark in the Cendrarian studies.

LOVEY, JEAN-CLAUDE. *Situation de Blaise Cendrars.* Neuchatel: A la Baconnière, 1965. A belabored effort to project Cendrars's humanistic grasp of the twentieth-century spirit. Stolid and frequently critically unsound.

MILLER, HENRY. *Blaise Cendrars.* Paris: Denoel, 1951. Trans. of the following articles by François Villié: "Tribute to Blaise Cendrars," *T'ien Hsia* (Shanghai), Vol. 7, 1938, rpr. in *The Wisdom of the Heart.* New York: New Directions, 1941, pp. 151–58; "Blaise Cendrars," in *Books in my life.* New York: New Directions, 1952, pp. 58–80. The most illuminating essays written on Cendrars in English. The personality of the man and the essence of the work are projected in a succinct and forceful manner.

PARROT, LOUIS. *Blaise Cendrars.* With selection of texts and a bibliography

by Jacques Henry Levesque. Paris: Seghers: Poètes d'aujourd'hui,
1948. Now outdated, this introduction to the man and his works
provides some perceptive insights. A landmark in Cendrarian criticism.

POUPON, MARC. *Apollinaire et Cendrars.* Archives des lettres modernes,
No. 103, Minard, 1962. A short monograph on the controversy over
the influence of *Zones* on *Pâques.* Well documented but not conclusive.

RICHARD, HUGHES. *Dites-nous, Monsieur Blaise Cendrars.* Lausanne:
Editions Rencontres, 1969. An anthology of Cendrars's interviews in
the French press (1919–1957) with annotations and a preface. This
interesting document would be of greater value if references of the
sources were given.

———— *Sauser avant Cendrars.* Revue Neuchateloise, 23rd year, No. 89
(Winter 1979-80). This monograph on the early years of Blaise Cendrars when he was still Freddy Sauser contains definitive and revealing
information on his family and the circumstances in which he was sent to
St. Petersburg with a duly obtained passport.

ROUSSELOT, JEAN. *Blaise Cendrars.* Collection Témoins du XXe siecle,
Editions Universitaires, 1955. A sympathetic introduction to Cendrars's works. Stronger on poetry than on prose works.

T'SERSTEVENS, A. *L'homme que fut Blaise Cendrars.* Paris: Denoël, 1972.
Interesting, pithy, and at times revealing comments on the personality
of Cendrars.

2. Special issues of periodicals

Livres de France, Hachette, Aug.-Sept. 1950.
Risques, "Salut Blaise Cendrars," No. 9–10, 1954.
Livres de France, Hachette, March 1956.
Les Ecrivains Contemporains, Innothera, No. 27, Feb. 1957.
L'Arc, No. 14, April 1961 (almost entirely devoted to Cendrars).
Hommage à Blaise Cendrars, Institut Français de Florence, Rome, Edi-
tions Luca, 1961.
Mercure de France, No. 1185, May 1962.
Europe, No. 566, June 1976.
Cendrars aujourd'hui, présence d'un romancier, L'Icasothèque 4, le plein
siècle No. 1, Minard, 1977.
Sud, "Cendrars vivant," No. 26, summer 1978.
Studies in Twentieth Century literature, Vol. III, No. 2. (Spring 1979).

3. Chapters in books and articles of special interest not previously mentioned

ASTRE, GEORGE ALBERT. *"Cendrars et la contemplation,"* Critique, V, No.
38 (July 1949), 662–64.

BARRET, ANDRÉE. *"Blaise Cendrars et l'esprit nouveau,"* *Europe*, No. 421–22 (May-June 1964), pp. 137–46.

BERGMAN, PÄR. *'Modernolatria' et 'Simultaneita': recherches sur deux tendances dans l'avant-garde littéraire en Italie et en France à la veille de la première guerre mondiale.* Upsala: Studia Litterarum Upsaliensia, No. 2, 1962.

CAWS, MARY ANN. *"Blaise Cendrars: a Cinema of Poetry,"* *The Inner Theatre of Recent French Poetry.* Princeton: Princeton University Press, 1972, pp. 25–51.

DOS PASSOS, JOHN. *"Homer of the Transsiberian,"* *Orient Express.* New York: Harpers, 1927, pp. 155–67.

EPSTEIN, JEAN. *"Le phénomène littéraire,"* *L'esprit Nouveau*, No. 9 (June 1921), pp. 965–69 and No. 10 (July 1921), pp. 1088–92.

FRANK, NINO. *"Blaise Cendrars, l'homme le plus seul au monde,"* *Les Nouvelles Littéraires* (December 21, 1929), p. 5.

————. *"Une mort difficile,"* in *Mémoire brisée.* Calman Lévy, 1967, pp. 209–25.

————. *"Bruit et fureur chez Blaise Cendrars,"* *Les Nouvelles Littéraires* (February 27, 1969), p. 6.

————. *"Blaise Cendrars, le mal aimé,"* *Les Nouvelles Littéraires* (January 28, 1971), pp. 1, 10.

FRICKER, BERNARD. *"Un héros moderne,"* *Sous le pavé la plage*, Bulletin de l'Association l'Agrafe d'or, No. 1, 1974, pp. 12–16.

GAUCHERON, JACQUES. *"Fernand Léger et Blaise Cendrars,"* *Europe*, No. 508–509 (August-September 1971), pp. 96–104.

GOFFIN, ROBERT. *"Blaise Cendrars et son influence,"* *Entrer en poésie.* Gand: A l'Enseigne du Chat qui Pêche, 1948, pp. 159–70.

————. *"Blaise Cendrars ce précurseur,"* *La Revue Générale Belge* (February 1961), pp. 63–71.

————. *Fil d'Ariane pour la poésie.* Paris: Nizet, 1964. Pp. 190–201 on Cendrars and Apollinaire.

HORREX, SUSAN. *"Blaise Cendrars and the Aesthetic of Simultaneity,"* *Dada-Surrealism*, No. 6 (1976), pp. 46–58.

LAGRUE, PIERRE. *"Guillaume et Blaise, poètes contemporains,"* *Europe*, No. 451–452 (Nov.-Dec. 1966), pp. 118–24.

LEROY, CLAUDE. *"Cendrars, bourlingueur ou une malle à double fond,"* *Cahiers du XXè siècle*, Klinsieck, No. 2 (1974), pp. 121–43.

————. *"Cendrars, le futurisme et la fin du monde,"* *Europe*, No. 551 (March 1975), pp. 113–20.

————. *"Cendrars et le tombeau du lecteur inconnu,"* *Littérature* Larousse, No. 27 (October 1977), pp. 35–43.

LE ROUGE, GUSTAVE. *Le mystérieux Docteur Cornélius.* Paris: Union Générale d'Editions, 10/18, 1975. Prefaces by Jean Hamon (Vol. I), Blaise Cendrars (Vol. 3), Francis Lacassin (Vol. 4), and Raymone Cendrars (Vol. 5).

LEVESQUE, JACQUES HENRY. "Blaise Cendrars" in "La galerie des contemporains," La Revue Nouvelle, No. 30 (May 1927), pp. 52–62.

MALRAUX, ANDRE. "Des origines de la poésie cubiste," La Connaissance, No. 1 (January 1920), pp. 38–43.

MANOLL, MICHEL. "Supplément à mes entretiens avec Blaise Cendrars. Les cent figures d'un sans culotte de la poésie," Arts, No. 364 (June 19–25, 1952), p. 7.

PARINAUD, ANDRE. "La peinture et ses témoins," Arts, No. 333 (November 16, 1951), p. 1.

————. "Blaise Cendrars, les foules modernes traversent la vie dans les passages cloutés," Arts, No. 368 (July 17, 1952), pp. 1, 6.

RICHARD, HUGHES. "Blaise Cendrars s'en va-t-en guerre," Journal de Genève, No. 229 (October 2–3, 1965), pp. 3, 5.

————. "Cendrars ou la volonté du mythe," Lettres Nouvelles (December 1969-January 1970), pp. 105–14.

RICHTER, MARIO. "Les Pâques à New York de Blaise Cendrars," La crise du logos et la quête du mythe. Neuchatel: A la Baconnière, 1976, pp. 63–95.

ROUSSEAUX, ANDRÉ. "La poésie brute de Blaise Cendrars," Le Figaro Littéraire (September 7, 1957), p. 2. Rpr. Littérature du vingtième siècle. Paris: Albin Michel, 1958, Vol. 6, 92–101.

ROUSSELOT, JEAN. "Blaise Cendrars ou l'état de légitime légende," Présences contemporaines, Nouvelles Editions Debrosse (1958), pp. 197–210.

ROY, CLAUDE. "Blaise Cendrars et Henry Miller," L'homme en question. Paris: Gallimard, 1960, Vol. 3, 288–96.

SIMENON. GEORGES. "Simenon écrit à Cendrars," Nouvelles Littéraires, No. 1736 (December 8, 1960), p. 1.

SOMVILLE, LEON. Devanciers du Surréalisme. Genève: Droz, 1971.

SOUPAULT, PHILIPPE. "Mort d'un poète," Revue de Paris (March 1961), pp. 158–60.

SZITTYA, EMILE. "Blaise Cendrars ou l'inquiétude de la fin du siècle," Lettres Françaises, No. 865 (March 2–8, 1961), p. 4.

Index

DATE DUE